T0413366

SICK AND TIRED OF BEING
SICK AND TIRED

Sick And Tired Of Being Sick And Tired

Written by:

Barbara J. Ross

To order additional copies of this book, contact:
Xlibris Corporation
1-888-795-4274
www.Xlibris.com
Orders@Xlibris.com
95220

CONTENTS

ACKNOWLEDGEMENTS

FAMILY MEMBERS, MY BELOVED MOTHER MAMIE MOTES, TWIN BROTHER BOBBY MOTES, SONS, ERNEST MOTES, ODIS DESEAN ROSS, MY SISTER, DELORIS NELSON, NEPHEWS, BRYON, BERRY NELSON, CO-WORKERS, YVETTE SPENCER, YVETTE BIBBS, ELVA PANTOJA, KAREN POPE, FOR THEIR ASSISTANCE WITH BOOK COVER AND FLOWER. DR. GREEN, MS. COLLEEN WALKER, MRS. JOANN ROSS. FRIENDS, MRS. RUSSELL, ERNEST RUSSELL JR, MY PRAY PARTNER RUTHIE WILLIAMS. DR. SUSAN KHLIEF, PROFESSOR—BAHEEJ KHLEUF.

INTRODUCTION

THIS IS A STORY OF A YOUNG WOMEN WHO HAD A LOT OF THINGS TO HAPPEN IN HER LIFE. WHAT BETTER WAY TO GET RIDE OF IT THEN TO PUT IT ON PAPER. SO IN THE MIST OF HER STRUGGLES SHE BEGIN TO POUR OUT WHAT WAS INSIDE, AS SHE TRYS TO FIND HER WAY OUT OF THINGS THAT OCCURRED, OR EVEN THINGS SHE MIGHT HAVE GOTTEN HER SELF INTO.

IN THE PROCESS SHE WOULD DISCOVER WHAT IT MENT TO LIVE LIFE ON LIFE TERMS THE GOOD AND THE BAD WITHIN HER SELF AS WELL AS OTHERS. IT IS IN THIS BOOK THAT SHE WOULD DISCOVER THE WISDOM AND KNOWLEDGE OF HOW THINGS CAN AND WILL ACCURE IN THE NATURAL AND IN THE SPIRIT.

CHAPTER ONE

INNOCENSE

As Angel sat in a smoke filled room she begin to travel back in time trying to find out where she might have went wrong and trying to find out what she needed to do to make things better. Angel begins to remember the time when she was about two years old she could remember when they lived in a basement apartment on 40th Ave and Langley. She was outside sitting down on the ground. She could still hear her mother's voice in the back of her mind telling her the story of how she started walking. Her mother never told her that, because she was being lazy about walking she had to take a switch and whoop her to make her start walking. Angel could not remember much of what happen to her from the age of two until she was about Seven. But she did remember that they would move a couple houses down the street into a two flat building on the second floor. Which was bigger and had more bedrooms. As Angel remembered; her mother ever slept in a bed but always on the coach. It was during this time she would have to share a bed with her sister and she really did not want to because her sister snored. What else she remember as she begin traveling back in time was that one day while her and her twin brother were out in the back of the house playing, her brother who had just clam that fence and she behind him, was now ready to come down. And after telling her once to move because he had to pee, she refused and it was only after the second time of him asking her and she refusing again that he pulled out him self and peed in her face. This was one of the funniest but not so funny at the time, things she would have to experience in her life. It was also at this time Angel would remember the time when she followed her twin brother and some of his friends to a place she knew nothing about, and in the process of following them they some how got a way from her and she could not find her way back home. Even though she was only about six or seven blocks from home and not knowing she was scared and it could not hurt to try and find her way back home or even ask some one as if they would know. So she went into a basement store and told the man in the store that she was lost and could not find her way home. So he called the police and they would help her find her way home. After driving up and down a couple of blocks, she would see the place where she lived. So they would stop, got out the car and take her to her mother she was glad. But boy was her brother in trouble. Looking back on it now the place was a building that she and her family would one day be living in call the projects.

Angel was now beginning to grow and she would now go through some of life hard walks the good and the bad. Angel would have to face life and its difficulties as they were. Still sitting in a smoke filled room Angel remembers when she was nine years old. At this age Angel would begin to develop breast and in the process of this stage in life it would bring grief of sexual abuse and Angel life would now change. There were times in Angel life when she would wish she were never born. She would remember when one of her Brother's friend would come down to their house, and in the mist of watching TV he would ask for a drink of water. The first thing her brother would do is tell her to go and give him some water. He would follow her to the kitchen to get the water and in the mist of getting the water he would feel on her breast and grind on her, so she would push him away and leave him standing in the kitchen. Angel to this day could feel the remorse she felt then now. This was not the only time Angel would have to experience this with this guy. Angel was friends with this guy sister so once in a while her mother would let her go down to Tiny's house. One particular night while she was spending the night down there; as she laid in the bottom bunk bed sleep; she all of a sudden felt something, and when she awoke to her surprise he was on top of her with his hand over her mouth and his other hand on his penis trying to put it in her. But his sister woke up in time and asked him what was he doing and he got up and left. Angel never told anyone what was happing to her by this guy in hopes that it would all go away. Not only that if she had of told her brothers what was happen to her by this guy they would have kill him. Only God knows what Angel would have to go through. Angel would have to bury a lot of things inside, as life would go on because she had no one she could talk to or any one that she could trust. Angel was the seventh child out of the nine children her mother gave birth to. With her being the seventh child, because she had a twin and a younger brother.

Well as time went on Angel and her family would have some times from what she could remember. She begin to remember the time when her mother had her brother tied to a tree and whooped because he stole some money from her. Not only that she remembered the time when her mother sold French fries for a quarter in the neighborhood to bring extra money in as well as working from time to time in a restaurant a couple of blocks down the street and around the corner. Angel mother did a lot of things to support the family. She could see the time when her mother would take them to church on Sunday morning. Also, Angel remembers when her mother had to comb her hair as a kid. Angel hated it because of the texture of her hair it was nappy, especially after it was washed. Then she could also still remember the time when her mother made her sister wash her hair and her sister tried to skull her head with hot water that was just one of the trouble days Angel would have. Many other thrilling and exciting things happen while they live on this block but she did not have that kind of time to tell them all.

Well Angel mother moved to another apartment after living in this apartment for some time. But only this time it was on 43rd and Rail Road street in a two-bedroom apartment not many of her brothers where living with them now. Still sitting in a smoked filled room she begin to travel to the age of ten and eleven when they lived on the first floor of this apartment. Sexual abuse in her life as she know it to be defined was still taking place but only this time it would be her family members. Angel was now in the hall way of the apartment sweeping the hall way floor when her uncle walked in, as she gave a hello, it would be then that he would approach her while she was sweeping the floor and felt on her breast, Angel was very upset and jerked away leaving him standing there. The last thing she could think was why was this man doing this he was her uncle! How could he do this kind of thing? This wouldn't be the only encounter of sexual abuse she would have while living in this house.

It would accrue again one day while sitting in her mother front room of the same house Angel remembers her older brother calling her to come and get some candy. And after hearing the words candy she headed back to the room where he was; once she entered the room he stood over her and told her to lay on the bed and helping her to lay down, he go on top of her. Not actually putting him self inside of her, but getting his rocks off and letting her up telling her to never tell anyone and given her a piece of candy. Angel leaves the room in tears and wonders to her self what is these people problem. How could this be happen to her, how could family members be doing what they where doing. Didn't these people realize that they had to see her face every day until they were gone? Did they not realize she was their little sister or niece did they even care. It was also at this time that she would realize that life had no remorse. Angel was now even more puzzle about life, she had some question in her mind about was it something she had done wrong or was something wrong with the people she know as family. She told no one of these two incidences that happen to her while they lived in this apartment as in the other apartment before this one. Angel had to now figure out some things; who could she tell, who could she talk to and when she thought about it, she really had no one she could trust or any one that she could talk to. Angel did not let this have no affect on her life. But she did hope that it would all go away and never happen again. During this time Angel gain a few friends in the area where she lived and there where time when she followed her brothers back to the old neighborhood.

She for a moment had a reflection of when her twin brother and one of his friend killed a bird, and they sat and discussed what God would do to people that hurt his animals. She became afraid for them hoping that God would for give them for what they had done, in hopes that they would never do it again. Angel purposed in her heart that she would never hurt or harm any of God animals.

It was during this time Angel begin to discover that she had feeling for one of her brother friends and he had feelings for her, his name was Lucus he was dark and kind of built at the time they where only about eleven. They had been friends all the time. And every now and then her and her brother would go over to his house and he would come over and sit with her at her house if her brother was not around in the kitchen. Angel mother did not mind plus adults know how it was when it came to having a first love sort of speak. This puppy love only lasted for a short time; but Angel thought she would make the best of it; considering what she had been through. Even as a young girl Angel could see that life was not just a bed of roses and the days ahead could be long.

One day Angel mother sent her to the store to get some what to this day she could not remember but because she would not find the store that her mother told her to go to, she went back home and when she told her mother that she could not find the store her mother told her oldest brother to whoop her and boy that is just what he did whoop her with a belt and it left scares on the back of her legs. From that day forward when her mother told her to do some thing she would do it to the best of her ability. So she would never have to be whooped again by any one.

After living on this block for about two years Angel brothers and one sister where now fading off and the family household where becoming lesser and lesser. Angel sister had gotten married and gone to live with her husband to another state because he was in the service. A couple of her brothers had went to live with their girlfriends so they could be on their own. Angel at this point could remember very few happy days, but she knows she has some. Angel remember their father coming over every now and then and given her and her brother a few dollars and he even took them to his house once in a while, but she never disliked him because of the few times he would spend with them. She would just enjoy the moments. She remember him coming over and drinking with her mother and seeing how happy her mother would be, so it made her happy. Not only that she loved her father. In the feature she would get to spend some more time with him, as he would go through some things, even up until his death.

On the weekends she was allowed to go and visited her grandmother and spends some time with her so this gave Angel some time to get away. Angel went to school down the street. Woodson North was the name of the school; and even at the school she did not have very many friends. What she remember the most about the school she was going to was her science class and in this class she learn that we have cold blooded and warm blooded animals. This texture of blood explains how animals survive in the summer and winter months. And she remembers the high school across the field where the teenagers went; call Forestville. Were the grammar school kids could go and get cookies; butter cookies. And kids from our school would go there every chance they had money. But the best of the worst was yet to come for Angel.

Angel who was now in the day coming into the future. To this day she could not understand why they where always moving but she guest it was do to lower rent prices, because they where on the verge of moving again, and they would now be moving in the same area where her grandmother was now living. So it would not have to be only on the weekends that she could see her grandmother, but she now could go to her grandmother house every day. But before she would reach this point Angel remember how they would catch the bus over to her grandmother house and one time her brother almost got hit by a car as they cross the street. And on another time when they where taking in a car she got her hand massed in the door, but to her surprise none of her fingers got broke.

She still remember some of the things her grandmother had to go through because one of her uncles that live with her grandmother was shell shock because he had been in the army and from time to time he would go off on my grandfather if he made him angry. So one day my grandfather made my uncle made and boy he chased him out of the house with a knife and my mother and other uncles and grandmother had to stop him. When I think about it; it was funny but it wasn't then.

I remember on this block we even thought it was a big block when had other family members that lived on this block my grandmother lived on my cousins lived in a basement apartment across the street from my grandmother and I could play with my cousins when I came over if my grandmother did not have me doing any thing. One of my oldest cousin was still peeing in the bed and they and I would hear the family talking about it. But it was about to be where Angel would not have to catch the bus or a car she and I would be down right across the street soon.

But what appeared to be looking better would only look better but would not feel better as time would go on.

It was now 1971, Angel was now about twelve years old; and they where now living on 57th Ave and Nowood in a two flat apartment building on the first floor in a two-bedroom apartment again. In the future Angel would now be able to make a little money for her self by baby sitting for the lady up stairs. Angel knew that her mother was doing the best that she could for her kids. And being on welfare it was not easy to buy for five kids. So any little bit counted even if it was candy money or a pair of shoes. She remembers the time when she could go to the shopping mall on 63rd street and buy two pairs of shoes for ten dollars. Then things where cheap and a person could get more for their money at that time. It would also be around this time that she would hang with some of the girls on the block and they would go to the mall and steal, yes. Angel remembers the one time she even took a ring. But was sure to never do it again.

Living in this area would be more favorable for Angel because she would be around more friends and family. She could remember the time when she and her cousin had a fight in the church van. Angel was getting to know about God and spirituality, she even sang in the church choir. This would be a time she would never forget because her cousin would get the best of her and not only that her cousin had a problem at that time. To this day she could not remember what cause this action to take place it happen and there was nothing any body could say or do to stop it. But angel mother would bar her cousin from their house for a while.

At this time Angel was interested in one of her brother friends and this time she was not being forced. She still could remember his name Dan.

Angel could remember this very well. Angel and his sister us to walk to school together, because at this time when kids wanted to fight you they would tell you at 3:00 o'clock they where going to get you. And during this time Angel had days she would be pick on because she was skinny and had a long neck. But when she came home he would come to she her at least that is what she wanted to believe. It is amazing how we can create a false sense of reality in our mind. Not really knowing what the other person is thinking or feeling Angel thought.

Because he was a little bite older than she was but it did not make her any difference; even though she was still in grammar school. Was she ready to let go of her innocents? She still remember the time when she had her first encounter of trying to experience what sex was like without being forced; so she thought. It was one day when her and one of her brothers were going to one of his girlfriend's house who lived just across the street. When the four of them went into her basement and lay on a mattress and processed by kissing and grinding and when it was time for him to put him self inside of her; he could not proceed and she was glade. The both of them got up and pull their clothes up and left never to tell any one. This so call relationship between the two of them did not last very long. Angel enjoyed the little time she spent with him because this was the second time she had felt something like this. It was then that she realized that love could be a beautiful thing if it is with the right person. But little did she know that finding the right person would take some time and she would have to go through a lot of things to get to that point of finding the right person. If there was ever a right person for her.

It was here in this area that Angel would start her first real relationship. Angel grandmother stayed down the streets now; so Angel could go and visit her grandmother at any time as she stated before. While one day Angel was on her way to her grandmother house for her mother, there was a young boy sitting on his porch as she passed he would speak and she would speak back. Not knowing that these hellos would lead to a relationship.

Angel spent many great times down her grandmother house as long as her cousin was not there because all she like to do was fight. She could remember the times when her grandfather was living and the movie Creature Feature came on; she would scare her grandfather by making deep sound from her voice that would scare him and he would call mudear that was Angel grandmother name; or at least that is what we call her for life. Not only that she could remember times when she would sit and chew tobacco with her grandmother and spit the juice in a can. Doing this made Angel feel grown. The time Angel spent with her grandmother where great times she learned many things from her grandmother. She learned to cook, clean, and do things in the garden, sew and make quilts; making quilts was her grandmother favorite. Angel would take some her frame of mind from her grandmother.

When it came to staying out of trouble and trying to do the right things.

At the age of twelve Angel would pick up a habit that would be hard to get rid of and that would be smoking. She could see her self-standing in the front of a garage with the rest of the girls taking a pull off of a cigarette that one of her other girls friend had. She could still remember that taste that it gave her for the first time; and it made her sick but she did not stop there. But she could hear her friend voice saying that the more you do it the better you would get. And that is what she did; the more she keep on trying the better she became but it would be a long time before she would let any one know what she was doing. At the age of twelve Angel had now got acquainted with Eric the boy that she was speaking to and they where now spending time together. Angel mother had now moved again but this time it was in the house her grandmother lived. And her grandmother had now moved down the streets on 57th and Union.

Her cousins, lived in the basement across the streets. Eric and Angel where getting to know each other and the more time she spent with him the more she got to know about him. She found out that they where the same age; and the same sign and they even went to the same school. Angel was now beginning to find out what it was like to be in a real relationship. This would be the beginning of Angel strife of trial and tribulation she would have to face. But Angel was ready, so she thought. But was she really ready for the things that were about to come her way.

Eric and Angel begin to spend time together; at the age of twelve, and Angel would spend more time down Eric house then at her own because her mother was drinking at this time. Angel will never forget the day that she started her menstrual cycle. She was playing outside one day when she went in the house to use the bathroom she found that there was blood all in her underwear. So she went and told her mother in which was not the best thing but the right thing. And after telling her mother; her mother went and told all most every body in the neighborhood. Angel had never been so embarrassed in her life. Not only that she had to go to the store and get some Kotex to put on; at this time this was the only thing her mother know about. But Angel will never forget the feel that bartered her the most about Kotex; which was the thickness in the pads that showed. She did not want people to know when she was on and with the pads it was not hard to tell. But as time went on she would be introduced to some tampons in the feature but until then she had to make the best of things.

Angel remembers something's that she really did not care to remember but was still fresh in her mind. Angel sister had now moved back to Chicago and was living down the streets around the corner with her husband and two kids she had now. She remember the time when her brother in-law friend tried to grind on her while she was baby-sitting for her sister. For some time this grown man call his self liking her even though she was just a young girl, what these men saw in Angel she would never know. As she look back on it now could it have been that she was to naive, or not out spoken enough so they took advantage it. So she thought she would tell some one. But the one time she would tell, she would get talked about. The day it happen she went and told her mother the one person she thought she could talk to. But after telling her mother she found out how drinking will make you say things that you might not mean to say to your children. Even though she know her mother loved her it was at this time that she felt abandon by her and that she did not love her; but this to would have to pass. During this time other attempts where made even in her own house but Angel vow to tell no one. She would just have to handle things for herself. But little did she know that things would get no better. She would not even tell Eric whom she was now drawing closer to.

But while these things where going on in Angel life she was working at becoming a better smoker when no was around because she had her own room now. Which give her time to think and try to find out why life was the way it was and the people in it.

She remembered this one guy which was her brother friend who lived next door liked her but she could never bring her self to like him. There was something about him she just did not like about him, he was not ugly or any thing she thought it might be his teeth that bartered her most, and he was older but she could never tell him that and even until this day when she see him he is still talking about the same thing, and she never give it thought. All she know is that she would never cheat on Eric even at this young age.

Time was passing by now and Eric and Angel where one now. They spent most of there time together. She remembers where-ever Eric was she was and where she was Eric was most of the time. When they where not hanging out with there other friends on the block. They went to the same grammar school; John Hope; where they would spend two years together and graduate together.

Attending this somewhat of a Junior High school was preparing them for when they got to the real high school. It offered course that a high school would. Angel enjoyed her times at this school and having friends was not that bad, except when trouble started. Living on this block has some good and bad times.

Angel and Eric seem like the perfect match people thought and so did Angel. Angel never did stop to think what her mother thought about what was going on but she never expressed any negative feelings about it either. Eric mother did not like the ideal at first, so Angel felt but as time went on she would adjust because Angel was not going to give up on Eric.

Angel felt a sense of peace being with Eric to the point she even though that may be some of sexual abuse would even stop if people saw that she was in a relationship with some one, and it did stop men from feeling on her, but it did not stop them from liking her.

Angel mother would soon move again and Angel would soon move with her sister onto what would be a family block on Union. Fifteen years had passed even in Angel mind still sitting in this smoked filled room. Angel was now remembering the day she and Eric graduated from grammar school. Angel would baby sit to earn some money to buy her something to wear for the lunching and graduation along with what her mother an sister would help her out with. What Angel remember best was that she was now living with her sister and the school was right down the street. Living on this block of 57th and Union wold have it memories also. It was as if two or three generations was living on this block. Her great grandmother and grandmother lived in the building on the corner, and her oldest brother lived with his girlfriend on the second floor of this building, we could walk out the back door and be right at their house. Angel had a big family. Angel could remember the time when the girl cousin that live next door to Eric them wanted to fight Angel; so one day when Angel was leaving from Eric house the girl followed Angel to her house and told her to come out and fight. So Angel did just that came out and fought and in the mist of the fight; Angel some how managed to pull the girl blouse off along with her bar and every one was looking at her; and not only that even though Angel did not have any long nails the girl face was scratch up how she will never know, all she knew was that she was fighting for her respect and the people that was watching the fight and she won. Because it got the girl off her back and she never bartered Angel again. This would be one of the times she would remember.

Angel and Eric and her twin brother would not be in grammar school long within two years they would graduating going on to high school. Angel and her twin where two different people, she looked like her mother and he looked like their father and had his ways. Angel tried to have a close relationship with him but it did not last long. You know how some twins would dress alike and do things together. This twin relationship was nothing like that she hardly ever saw him and even though they did graduated from high school. He begins to do things that would get him into trouble and he went to live with there mother while she stayed with her sister. Because if she was going to learn any thing she know she would have to learn it from her sister and so she stayed by her sister side along with Eric sisters too.

As a graduation present Angel sister husband took her and her twin Bobby and Eric to the show to see the movie coolly High; they had a great time that night. Her brother in-law went on to encourage her about how to set goals in life and finish high school and how not get pregnant and other things. Needless to say she took some of his advice.

As Angel set reflecting three years had passed in her mind and things seem as real as though it was happen as she reflected back.

Some would say that it is better to leave the past behind

In 1974, Angel and Eric were now in high school; Angel had heard a lot about the school from others that had went there, and now they where about to attend Tilden High School because many of their family members had gone and they could Tell some stories; racism was in the neighborhood where the school is located. Angel and Eric would spend four years at Tilden high and there would be changes in their life. Eric would pick Angel up in the morning for school and they would some time walk to school and walk home. What Angel would remember the most about being at this high school was the one evening when her and Eric and his best friend Wayne were on their way home after ninth period class; they saw a girl and two boy's sitting on a porch.

Angel felt as if something was about to happen; what she did not know was whether or not they would get away. So as they walk passed one of the boys said let's get them Niger's; and as soon as they passed that is when the trouble begin. They begin to chase them. Angel knew once they made it to the vilock that they would be find. Well they manage to get away; but angel was not pleased. She did not like the ideal of being chase by someone that was racist. Dr. King and those before him have set us free and we, as blacks because of the color of our skin should not have to go through this. During this time in Angel life a lot things would happen as a teenager. She could still remember the time when she went to help Eric sister sherry fight some girl that she said was messing with her; and in the mist of messing with the girl Angel got cut in the back while Sherry and her boyfriend stood by and watch. Lucky enough the cut was not that bad. And the next day Angel sister would take her to the doctor to get some stitches but they said that they should have come the same day. Angel still has the scare to this day. During this time Angel would draw close to Eric sisters even though Sherry did not like her very much; but she would not let that stop her and besides his mother and her seem to get along and that's what matter the most, not that she did not care about his sister that was her age that she got along with.

Angel loved kids and had been keeping kids for some time now. There would be times when she would find her self keeping her sister kids and then Eric sisters kids while they went out or had some place to go, some time she would get paid and some times she wouldn't but it would soon come a time when she would be having her own. Angel draw a close relationship with Eric older sisters because she had seven brothers and he five sisters, which meant that she could learn some things from his sisters as well as her own

Angel was now fitting in with the things that other people where doing and her innocence was now leaving.

Angel, one of God creation born innocent with inequities all around her soon finds out that innocence on this side does not last long. Inquities stands at the door awaiting to stripe you of all that God has for you. What do you do? Even in our innocence things will happen that we some time have no control over; so what do we do.

Just as the Bible talks about putting those things behind us; and reaching for our goals. What Angel learn to do; not that she did not think back on things that came her way but she learn to what the enemy meant for bad in her life and make it work to her good.

So often time people tend to hold on to things, which gives the enemy room. "To steal, kill and destroy" you with. It is these hidden things in our life that causes us as people to fall in the hands of the enemy. And we as human use it to drown our sorrows with drugs, alcohol, and other substance that make us bond and trap in the enemy hands; but I come to let you know if he did it for me he can do it for you. Stop given the enemy room in your heart and mind.

God told us in his word that he would "take the foolish things to confound the wise". Take what the enemy meant for bad and make it work to your good. I did because I am now telling my story every chance I get to help others. To let them know that they can make it because we are more than conquers through Christ that strengthen us.

If there is any young women or older women that is still struggling in this area of your life; I recommend that you turn it over to Jesus. Let go and let God heal you and deliver you for the past.

The things that loneliness, hopelessness and the desire to be loved can bring upon ones life, when you're young and don't know the troubles, heartaches and pain life can bring. Yet looking for love in all the wrong places and doing all the wrong things that it can and will bring. Evil lurking on every side being blinded by things that you can not see, and have no knowledge of. Will come upon you. It can only leave you wondering around for years trying to see what

God was really trying to tell me and you.

CHAPTER TWO

RELATIONSHIP

In 1975, Angel became pregnant by Eric in their second year of high school. Angel could still remember the day when her sister who she was still staying with and her mother came together to talk about what was going to happen. Angel sister and mother asked her what was she going to do and she told them that she was going to continue school and have the baby. One thing Angel was sure about was that she was not going to let nothing stand in the way of her education even if she did not make the best grades but was average. She did not know if Eric know she was pregnant so she told him.

Eric at the time was scared and did not know how his parents were going to take it. So while he was telling his best friend Wayne little did he know that his father was listening to them in the basement! Even though Angel had been through some things with Eric family it would take some time for them to really grow to like her, but things turns out for the best and Eric did what was right and that was to get a job and take care of his child. In the beginning of the pregnancy Eric had to watch Angel experience morning sickness.

Being pregnant was not a easy job for Angel she would have morning sickness there would be days when she did not want to go to school but she had to.

Angel sister would be moving soon and she would have to move back with her mother in the projects. The last thing Angel wanted to do was move with her sister and husband on the north side. A couple of months after finding out she was pregnant Angel moved to the projects with some changes that life would bring for her and Eric. By this time Angel and Eric would become distant; many things would get in the way of their relationship without them realizing it. Eric cared for Angel but when Angel realized it; it would be to late. Nine months has passed and Angel and Eric was still seeing each other but growing apart. She would see Eric at school and when he brought her home and some times she would go to his house.

What Angel remembers most about this pregnancy was when it came time for her to give birth. The funniest thing happen that night. Angel had got in labor that night and at first she was skeptical about telling her mother about the labor pains so she waited for a while before she told her. What really made Angel tell her mother she was in labor was when the last time she went to lay down in the bed to try to go to sleep she got one of the hardest pans that it took her some time to get out the bed on one side. So her mother sent up stairs to get her brother Reggie to take her. Reggie stayed up stairs with his girlfriend Debra so they came down stairs and got in the car. So once they arrived at the hospital; not realizing that they had went to the wrong door Reggie and Angel got back in the car and before Debra could get back in the car Reggie was driving off leaving her standing outside; until Angel had to remind him that he was leaving her. Angel laughed so hard that she could not believe she was in labor and laughing at the same time.

This labor would be the hardest labor she would have to go through. She would have to spend sixteen hours in labor before the child would decide to come out, through this again in the back of Angel mind all she could think of was that if she had to go through this again; she would make sure that the baby was ready and on its way out before coming to the hospital. Eric was not in the labor room with her but she know that her family would get in touch with him to let him know and the next day he would be there. Well it was July 13, 1976, and Angel finally gave birth to a baby boy, which look just like his father and his family. Some time before Angel had the baby, his family was saying that the baby was not his and Sherry his sister had some problems with whether or not it was his child. But the truth would be told; not only did he have their hair but also he had his completion and size. He would be the first born of three generations. Little Eric the third; when Eric found out he came to the hospital to see how Angel and the baby were doing. Things where okay for a while. But now changes would take place in their lives.

Angel continue to go to school while her mother baby sat. During this time Angel now felling the need to be on her own not that she did not like staying with her mother, but there where something's that were taking place in the home that she was concern about but there was nothing she could do. You see every one in Angel family drink. And some days would be better than others.

Angel and Eric would experience some physical and mental changes that life would bring on.

Six months after the first child Angel became pregnant again, but only this time she would get an abortion without Eric knowing. As Angel thought; could this be what caused them to fall apart. Angel remembers the day when her and one of her cousin went down town to get it. This event that took place would hunt Angel for the rest of her life. There would be times in Angel life when she would wonder what would this child have been a boy or girl; what part in her life would the child have played. But she would never know. Angel once read in a book that the children that did not make it in life would see their parent again in heaven. Because God takes those children and rise them up and use them in heaven because of the purpose they had whether it was for here or in heaven.

It was at this point that Angel life begin to change for the worst. Well as time went on Eric started cheating on Angel; but Angel had to admit that she had a crush on a guy that she had grow up with and she would go to see him and his mother every chance she got. But the sad part was that Angel was not sure about how he really felt about her or if he even felt anything for her. Even though there would be times when she would allow herself to be used by him. Angel was one that care for little negativity and wanted nothing to do with it. Even when it came to men she was not about to fight over no one. Especially a man, so she just played it by ear to see what was going to happen. Was Eric really doing what people said he was doing? What proof did she have that this was really happen! Even though she had a childhood cruse on some one that she had grow up with, he wasn't a family member; but who said she could not dream.

Well Angel would soon find out that it was true Eric was messing around with some one else when the girl would call her house. How did this girl get her phone number it must have been some of Eric sister sherry doing because they did not like her at the present time? So Angel would talk to Eric and tell him to tell her to stop calling her house; but even he had no control over what she said or did. So after this event Angel would start liking other men if he could do it so could she. Once a cheater always a cheater. Time had gone on and now Angel was ready to move out on her own. Angel was receiving welfare now and this would be money that would help her get her own apartment. Not only that she was afraid that something bad would happen one day between her brothers and she did not want that to happen. So Angel would get her own apartment.

She would also remember the time when she left Eric Jr. in the bed while she went down stairs for her mother, and when she returned and went in the room to check on him she couldn't find him, but seconds later when she looked under the bed there he was laughing. Angel had never been so scared in her life. But he was okay.

Angel mother had been drinking and she had not heard any thing and Angel assumed that her mother had not even went in there to check on him while she went down stairs for her.

Then there was the time when two of her brothers had been playing cards for money and because her twin was a sore looser he got mad and wanted to fight her other brother. And went and got a sick to hit him in the head with, the only thing that stop it was her. Angel had to watch her mother go through many things within her self as well as with the children she had raised.

Angel went out and got an apartment for her and her son but Eric would come and live with them. Angel moved in a basement apartment on 52nd Street and fourth Ave. It was a one bedroom apartment that one of her brother had moved out of and told the landlord who was an elderly lady and man couple.

After talking with them Angel would get the apartment and move as soon as possible. Angel had a apartment that she could call her own. Eric lived with her and he worked. Angel and Eric was still in school; so what she would do is take the baby over to her mother or his mother house for the week and pick him up on the weekend or sometimes Eric mother would keep him. Eric mothers love Angel and Eric Jr. as well as his father and treated them with kindness. Angel loved going over to Eric mother house because his mother cooked just as her mother did no matter what, it was just apart of the old fashion way of life for them and having as many kids as they did to feed. So Angel know she could always get a meal when going over there.

Living in this apartment brought Angel and Eric some good days and some bad. During this time Angel would get closer to his older sisters Lena and Die, and Pudding because it appeared that she got along better with them. Angel at this time was in the age where she and Eric could go out and drink and that is what they did most of the weekends was either go to his mother house or go out. But they would have some good times; until her or Eric would mess it up. Angel could remember some of the time she had in this one bedroom apartment. She could see and remember while Eric lived with her what it was like. She still could see fresh in her mind the time when Eric got his first jerry curl put in his head. He look nice with it, but it also made it go to his head. In the long run Angle would get the same thing but the first time she got it done it did not turn out like she thought it would. She don't know if it was because she let his sister do and she did not do it right.

But before that Eric and Angel would go through some things like the time he brought the some women that was calling her at her mother house, Angel went to Detroit with her sister, but before they left Angle did every thing she needed to do. Like make sure the house was clean and made sure nothing was dirty. She even brought new clothes to take with her. They were only going for a weekend but Angel wanted thing to be right when she left. And besides Eric was acting kind of strange like he was ready for her to leave so that him and his friend could do what they wanted to do.

Angel knows that she was not going to let what she thought about Eric get in the way of her taking this trip. So she set her house in order and went. When it was time for her to return from the trip; she did not let Eric know when she was returning for the trip; she did would just return unexpected.

Angel senses some thing before she left but she let it go. Only to return to her home to find that Eric was not there and the house looked just like she expected. Eric had another woman in her house; how could he do this to her she thought. As Angel set in this smoked filled room she could still see the apartment as it was when she return from the trip. There where ashes piled in the ashtrays that had never been empty. Bed looking like some other woman had slept in it. She was angry but what could she do this is where it would all begin.

Angel waited for Eric to come home and she did not move anything; she left things just as she had found them to see what his response would be. Well as any one would know when Eric came home surprise to find out that Angel was at home and the house was still looking the same way he and his friend Chris had left it. All he could say was that him and Chris had been there and that if he had of known that she was coming home he would have clean up.

Angel was not going for that she know that some other woman had been in her house and now all she was waiting for was it to come out. Angel was not getting ready to feel some life hard knocks. Angel now had to figure out what she was going to do about the situation. As time went on the truth would come out about what really happen while she was gone out of town,

Angel would never for get the day Eric hit her for the first time in her life. It happens one Saturday after noon while she was over to his mother house. Sherry and Janie were now getting along again once she know he was cheating on her; but his other sister Janie who Angel got long with very well, the telephone rang and Angel pick up the phone and answered it in a way that one should answer with a hello. When the voice on the other end said may I speak to Eric and Angel asked who is this and the person on the other end said none of your business; let me speak to Eric. So Angel was determined that the person on the other end was not going to speak to Eric until she found out what she wanted to know. And that is when Betty the girl on the other end apparently got mad and begins to tell Angel every thing.

She call Angel a bitch and begin to tell Angel that she had been to her house; and that she had taking some things out of her house. The things she was saying Angel did not mind but when she told her she had taking some things out of her house Angel begin to get mad. She called Eric to the phone he know that he was in trouble now and there was know getting out if it. So by this time Angel proceeded out the door leaving Eric on the phone with Betty. As she begins to walk home Eric came around the corner in his car and pulled over telling her to get in the car. But she refusing to get in the car; after he had asked her twice. Eric got out the car and walked up to Angel and asked her one more time to get in the car and when she refused again; he howled off and slapped her in the face so hard that she saw stars with a ringing in her ears. So she got in the car and he got in and the whole time he was trying to apologize but Angel would not except it.

Angel knew that from this point on that if he hit her once he would hit her again. She was reminded of how his father did his mother and she did not want this to happen to her. Upon entering their house she begin to lash out at Eric and calling him names. And in the mist of this Angel ask the lord to give her the strength to bet this man so that he would know that you can not just go around hitting on woman because you are in the wrong or angry/bigger. In the mist of asking Angel some how to this day can not explain how she got her arms around his neck and begin choking him. She saw tears coming out of his eyes asking her again to let him go and he would leave and she let him go and he left. Angel and Eric had their first real brake-up, Angel was still in school; paying the bills with her Aid check and buying food for them to eat. How could he do this to her! Angel mother had taught her that there is more than one fish in the sea even though she liked Eric a lot and hope that they would one day get married.

Not only that Angel was looking for some one she could share her life with Eric was not a bad guy and every one made mistakes; but how long would it take Angel to realize this and would it be to late when she did.

From this point on in Angel life thing begin to become complicated it was as if she know what she wanted; but how could she tell who was the right man or what was the right thing to do. She would not know unless she tried it or went through it to find out. But what Angel did not know was what she was about to go through would leave her scared for the rest of her life. Angel begins to have other male friends. Angel would return to a old situation with the guy she grow up with and again he was not the one even though she would make a fool out of her self from time to time with him. He did not have a real entrance in her even though she still had a crush on him. There were some things she would do without realizing what she had done until it was to late. Angel was a strange person even to herself she often had to go back and figure something's out about herself. Even asking herself question of why and what to recall her action.

Angel never really got a relationship off the ground with Gray and it would take her some time before she would. But in the mean while Eric was not out of the picture. Even though Angel and him had there difference there was some things still there and it was not just the child. She and Eric would get together and breakup when things where not going her way. This was her way of getting even. They never had another fight after this; but like it was said if he hit you once that he would hit you again. And it did happen! One day when Eric had came over to her motherhouse to pick her up. Angel was at her mother doing the same things she usual do while over there and that was playing cards and drinking. But this particular day Gray was over there Eric was ready to go but Angel was not and she told Eric knew that he could go and plus she had been drinking. So Eric asked her to step outside her mother door and when she did he proceeded to try to talk to her and he saw that there was know taking to her. So he took his fist and howled off and hit her again.

She was stung she did not know what to do. Eric knows that it was over; what other way to build the male ego then to strict out at the person. We see it done all the time even in the home. What was now a dream would come to reality. Well after this Eric would get even with Angel and he did by going with her brother ex-girl friend who stayed down stairs. Angel was even angrier with Eric. But deep down inside there was something going on that both of them cared not to admit. They really loved each other in their own way but the problem was how do one express it and don't mind being real with yourself and others. Angel knows that her and Eric were both trying to be tough about what they were really feeling.

Considering this fact it would cause problems in the relationship. Life for Angel was now up in the air and what one man did not do another would; at least that is what she was taught; but Angel would find out that it is not always true. A person would probably have to go through a couple of men to find the one that would do.

Angel was one that would not worry about simplistic things such as this. If she did not know anything else; she know that men came a dime a dozen. Angel decided to let go and let God and if this was meant to be it would happen. She continued to finish school and go on with her life. Angel know what she was looking for in a relationship not knowing that she would go through something's to get what she was looking for it she ever found it. From this point Angel would go through some challenges; up and downs good times and bad times, happy times and sad times, lonely times. But she would have God through it all to bring her through and out of it. Some of the things Angel would face would be and unforgettable experience.

It was at this time Angel had to decide what she wanted out of life. She was sure she wanted to finish her education and work for a living. She was an independent person and if some one gave her it would have to be out of the goodness of their heart. With Angel she know something's was strange within her but she just could not put her hand on it. Even as a child growing up she could feel the present of the Lord with her, one thing Angel was sure of and that was what ever she went through and know matter how hard times got she was not acting at her best.

Angel remembers in the year of 1980, she worked her first job at Kiddee Krome where her sister worked. This company made little tables and chairs for kids. The job only paid 5:35 an hour; but it was a job and Angel would work until an accident happens that would cause her to leave. Angel could careless she still had public Aid to fall back on and to still pay her bills and rent.

Angel was still living in the apartment in the basement paying two hundred and fifty dollars. She spent most of her time alone but had company from time to time. Out of the men Angel knew they weren't what she wanted or was looking for, so she could not build a relationship with them. Sex for Angel was not a big thing and she did not have to have it. As Angel would find out most men are looking for one or two things any way and that it sex and a place to lay their head.

In the summer of 81, Angel life would make a complete turn around from what she was use to. Now Angel and Eric where now friends and had put their difference to the side. And even in the mist of hard time for Angel, Eric would be there for her. With out even thinking Angel felt it was time to move on and that her and Eric would always have some communication with each other because they had a son that they did have to raise despite their differences still again.

Angel know that Eric was trying to move on with his life because he was still seeing other women and she would now have to except it for what it was.

So it was at this time Angel would start what she though would be a new relationship new yes! But what the relationship would turn out to be would be another story.

What do you do when you find your self lonely and alone, confused and don't know what to do. Be careful when you find your self in this stated of mind because it will cause you to do and say things that are really not you; it's just your emotion that are over taking you. Causing you to go into place you don't want to go and doing things that could hurt you. Causing you to make what you believe to the right decision but wrong. Seeking things you know nothing about.

CHAPTER THREE

WHAT LOVE GOT TO DO WITH IT

One afternoon when Angel had left church she decided to stop by her sister house to see what she had cooked. Because by this time her sister and her husband had move back in the area into a house. Upon entering the house she saw this tall dark handsome man sitting in the dinning room of the house. Angel entered the dinning room and spoke with a hello! As he returned with a hello. Angel sister Debra introduced him; his name was Odie Rose. Even though this man was handsome; as she was looking on the table in which he and her was sitting there were liquor and beer cans on it. One thing Angel was not looking for was a alcoholic to spend the rest of her life with, but she would give him time to talk just to see what he was talking about and just how fare he would go with her. Well Angel spent most of the day at her sister house listening to this man talk about what he was and who he was and none of this meant any thing to Angel. This couple of hours of listening to this man talk; made Angel realize that this was not the man she wanted to spend the rest of her life with, but would she fellow her first mind or would she let her emotions get in the way of her future.

Still sitting in a world of past thoughts; it was as if Angel had recalled each moment as thought it was today. Even though Angel let Odie take her home that night she was sure that he was not the one. But who's to say what the future would bring. Because Angel was a person who had compassion for others more so than for herself. She allowed Odie to call her from time to time but that is as far as she wanted it to go; so she thought.

One night when Angel and her sister in law were going out they went to a lounge where Odie just happen to be. It was wintertime and there was plenty of snow on the ground. Angel knows she was not a real drinker but she went just because she was invited as always. They drank and talked and had a good time. Angel was very uneasy about being in lounges because any thing could happen and for some reason she just did not feel safe. It was not like when she was with Eric and his sister and they went out. This was much different she was with a stranger someone she hardly knew. Well the night had ended and the next day was coming in; and it was time to go home; Angel was not one that would stay out to let in the morning. So her sister in-law went home and left her and Odie sitting at the bar. So Angel told Odie she was ready to go home. Not to mention that he did not have a car at this time and they had to take the bus in all the snow. Angel like to froze but they made it. After arriving at Angel house she let Odie put the key in the door and do to the temperature the key broke off in the door and he had to brake the door in to get in the house. So it was that night in 81, when Odie and Angel started having a relationship.

It was here that Angel would get to know something about Odie and his family. His mother live down south with his father and sisters; which was where he was from. But he came up here to get a change of passe from the Mississippi life. Odie stayed with his aunt and uncle on the South East side of town; and he would take her over there to meet them. They were nice people even though the apartment they lived in was worn; you could tell they had been there for a long time and it was roach infested. She would never forget the time when she spent the night over there and the next morning she had roach bites all over her she vowed never to spend the night again no matter what.

Then she would meet his cousin who seems to be nice woman and man but they all drank. But she would never really build a relationship with them like she did with Eric and his family. Angel would find out that Odie was a ladies man and thought he had it going on with very little money in his pocket. But she knew that was not the case because he had never had his own place. And the job he worked on did not pay that much money. Even though he dressed his best and wore hats. One would guess he took that after his father. Who she would only get to meet one time.

From this point on trouble seem to be all around Angel. It was like hell had crack open and couldn't be close for a long time.

It was from that night that things would began to happen for Angel and Odie. Angel would see Odie from time to time and most of the time when she saw him he was drunk or drinking. Angel knew she would not be able to get use to this kind of behavior; but she thought she would give it a try. In the beginning of 82, Angel and Odie were still seeing each other somewhat. So one day Odie showed up at her house to inform her that he was going to the service. At first Angel thought that this man was joking and this was not a good ideal for her; but after some time thinking about it she figured that this might be what he need to stop or slow down his drinking. So she gave him encouraging words and told him that she would be there for him when he came home. But in the back of her mind Angel thought to her self if she could only take back what she said. Dispute what had happen before Eric and another guy she cared for to say.

Angel knew what she wanted and what she wanted to do and that was to settle down and raise a family and be happy. She hoped that she could find some one with the same goal" she had. She was not search of what she was looking for, but little did she know what she would be in search for would be a long time and some of it in fear and misery. Odie went to the service and Angel tried to do the right things just in case he should come back to get her. Even though doing the right thing don't always happen. Angle had to admit that she did do some things that were not right

But it was what it was. In July of 82, Odie did come back to marry her it happen in the strangest way for her. It happens in the strangest way for her after a night of lust she did not know what the next morning would bring. It happens one Saturday morning; it was a nice summer day had set in and Angel and Odie had awake from a long night. When Angel just in thought threw out the question to see what Odie response would be. Let's get married she said and his response was okay. Not really thinking that he was going to go through with it. He got up and put his clothes on and telling her to get ready. Needed she remind herself that this was just a spare of the moment thing and did she even mean what she had just said! With out giving it any thought Angel got dress to and not telling a soul except her brother Ronny who was staying with her; know one else knew. What would Eric have to say about this how would he feel about it? Knowing that he was the one she should have been marrying. Angel the whole time things where taking place could not believe that this was happing; it appeared that she was thinking and doing at the same time. But not wanting this to be happen. What was she doing! Stop!

Angel never stop to consider what Odie motives was for doing what he was doing but she would find out some time a head.

Even on the way downtown to the City Hall building there was this small still voice telling Angel this could be the worst mistake you have ever made in your life. Angel felt she should have told Odie to quite while they where a head but it would not come out.

What would he say to have come this far to stop now! To this day she will never know because she did not have the nerve to find out and it never entered his mind to ask. Angel last name had now change to Ross. She had just made a life time commitment to Odie one that would not be so easy to get out of even if she wanted to. A man now had papers on Angel; she would not only need a song but a prayer also. After the papers where signed and they where now married; they would go back and spread the news that they where married. She went by Eric motherhouse to let them know not that it made any difference to them because it was not there son that she was marring. Then she went and told her sister and the rest of the family. It was a sad but happy day and Angel would have to make the best of it; and the future she would find out the real reason why he did what he did.

It was at this time that Odie had to go back to the service but he would return to get Angel and Easton her four-year-old son. But that was not Angel problem that stood at the front of her mind, her biggest problem was could she let the past go. This meant that Angel would now have to give up the male friends she had; not that they had done any thing so great for her. This was one of the reasons why she got her self into this mess because she was trying to leave the pass behind. In a couple of months Angel and Odie would be moving to North Caroline where he was station.

It was the winter of 82, going into 83;Odie had come to get Angel and Easton. Angel would leave her one bedroom apartment and everything in it with her sister; because it was too costly to bring everything she had with her. Not knowing what was really going on. But she felt as if the move would clear the air of the pass men in her life. One-week later Angel and Odie and Easton would be taking the Greyhound bus to the base where they would be living. All the signs where there but some time we tend to look over the signs to follow our feelings. The bus rid would be a long one a twenty one-hour ride to be sure. It would be a ride to remember because Angel would get to see things that she had never saw before, and be in places she had never been in before. The ride was better than expected the bus made stops in Washington D. C and they took pictures and walk around until it was time to get back on the bus.

Often times Angel thought about did he have enough money to do what needed to be done? And had he taking care of thing like he was suppose to; she would soon find out.

Again the signs where there but Angel failed to see them for what they where. Because even on the trip they did not have enough money do eat with and enjoy themselves because he said he spent the money on the ring and moving cost of the what things she was taking with her.

Not only that he never told her how much money the service was paying him. Also, she would discover that he was sending his mother some money.

After arriving in North Caroline it was about two o'clock in the morning and it was cold. Angel just knew that she was about to go into a house where it was nice and warm and get into a nice warm bed. It was not so Odie had for got to get gas for the heater so they would have to sleep in the cold for the next couple of hours. This was just one of the signs as a give away to Angel. Because he said that he had everything ready. What was one night it wouldn't be so bad she thought. The next morning Angel called the gas people out to put some gas in the tank. In North Caroline things where nothing like Chicago everything is based on you getting and then paying for it. Not there you pay then you get. Angel and Odie had to pay for water, gas, and food. Angel just knew that Odie would have enough to take care of them as a family. But she would soon find out that it was not so. She would have to make ends meet like she did in Chicago. But at least she had family there she could go to. Things were not the way every one said it would be. Angel could still remember that first Christmas in North Caroline; she had nothing to give her son because they had no money to any thing with. Odie did manage to come up with one or two gifts for Easton. Angel was not happy at all but the worst was to come little did she know. Time was going on now and Angel decided that now would be a good time to get right with God; by reading his word and finding her a church home. Angel made some friends black and white.

The white ones seem to be a little more friendly than the black ones. Because we know how black people can be and how fast they will turn on you. It would be the black friends that she would pray and study the word with and it would be the white ones that she would hang around when she or they need some one to talk to. Either way it went she would not put any difference between the two. They would both be her friends she would make no exception on either side. Angel found a church that she could attend even on Wednesday nights just as if she was at home. The church body was mostly black; but she had gone to some white churches just to show that she was not prejudice about any one or anything. Angel was now trying to get in with God because she knows he was calling her and she was answering the call. Angel was a strange person because when it came to the things of God or act of God and not only him but the enemy to she was not afraid but it came as amazement to her to see the power of God at work. Little did she know that this is where she would conceive again; God would open her womb! In the mean time things started off okay with Odie he was letting Angel handle the money and take care of the bills. She should remember the times when she got up at four and five o'clock in the morning just to iron his uniforms just so he could look good going to work.

The joys of being married would only last for a while; and it would be much different then she though it would be. After about three months Angel marriage would go down hill. Odie would start drinking even heavy then before. Angel would never know what the problem was, that was causing him to drink and act the way he was. But it wasn't as if she didn't know this from the beginning.

Angel still stilling in a smoke filled room she could remember some event of the past as thought it was yesterday. The church Angel was now attending was a big church on the outside that sat on the corner of the street a block or two from where they were staying and Angel could walk there and back in no time. Most of the places a person wanted to go you would need a car or walk which were some long walks there and back. It was also during this time that because Angel could not find a job she would spend most of her time getting to know God and his word.

Angel read the bible day and night trying to get to know God and his word. She knew she would need him more than ever and not only that she had been having a feeling that God was preparing her for something. She would not find out just what it was that God would have her to do. God would now show Angel his power and how he worked in the lives of his people, or people the good and bad. Angel was now ready to find out what it was God had in store for her.

She was willing to do the best of her ability what was right by God and only the devil would be mad. So Angel begins to get in the word and the word became alive in her soul. Now don't get her wrong this does not mean that she became a saint over night. But the more she read the word the more she had a mind to do the right things. But the enemy was mad with Angel now; so he would be out to steal, kill and destroy her in any way he could.

Angel knew that the enemy was out to get her and once in with God there could be no turning back. Because the word say that once a man has sweep and cleaned his house; and the enemy walk to and fro seeking rest and can't find any. He returns to the house that he has once lived; only to find it sweep and clean; trying to bring seven more spirits than before.

Angel had some ideal of what this meant but she would get the full effects of what this really meant. Angel husband was not staying out even though she had a few friends she could talk to; this could not make up for being in the house with no one to talk to. Being alone could not make up for not having some one to hold you or make love to you in your time of need. But it does leave room for the enemy to come in without knowing what affects he will leave behind. Even though Angel was now in to serving God this did not mean that the enemy would leave her alone as she would soon find out.

Some months had passed and things went well for a while long as the bills were paid and food was in the house and Odie wasn't drunk. But then there would come times when the bills would go half paid and there was little food in the house and Odie would not come in or if he did he would be drunk and tried. This is where Angel would have some of the worst experiences of her life some that would leave her scared for life. Some of the events that took place would always be fresh in the back of her mind.

After Angel had join the church and the Lord had filled her with the holy spirit; the gifts that God had for her would now come forward, but the enemy has some spirits he wanted to show her also. For example, Angel could remember the first time she got filled with the Holy Spirit in a dance; it was a feeling that can be explained. Her feet got light and this strange feeling begin to come over her and before she know it her body was moving in the form of a dance motion. This was a day that she would never forget. But than she also remember the time when she first saw a bad spirit in a woman and the demon was making noise. It happen one Sunday during a closing prayer and the anointing begin to fill the place and in the mist of the anointing this woman begin to start making this loud noise and grueling. At first every one started looking and still praying and then they begin to move the crowd back because these spirits are nothing to be playing with; and as she looked on this person you could see the spirit fighting not to come out of the woman and they were praying and putting oil on her to make it come out. But in the mist she found her self on the floor trying to get out of the way of it. Angel thought this was a sight for sore eyes to see; but it was an experience that she would not forget. Not only that she felt as if God was not only letting her see that demons are real, but also that they are nothing to play with.

Angel always know that these things were real but she had never had to experience seeing them in action except with what you see on TV. Angel would now learn how demons worked in the spirit realm through others and with the spiritual eye; she would learn how they move within a person inside and outside of a person. She would have to go through something's to get this experience. Angel was now seeing less of Odie her husband and the only friends she had were Cindy one of her white friends across the walk way and she know of some other people that were black that she could go and visited. But she would soon get tried of that. So she would sit in the house when she did not feel like going anywhere after she had got Easton off to school.

It would be at this time Angel would experience some thing's "that she had never had to experience seeing spirits in action, not quite like what one would see on TV. This spirit that would try to attach itself to her would be a spirit of masturbation. This spirit is seductive in the mind of a person and it causes one to act in a way that is not natural but unnatural when it is not with another human. So one can find her/him self caught in the grip of this spirit when looking for love or sex and there is no one to for fill the need.

A door to the reproductive system has been open. It was the summer of 83, when things had begin to change for Angel; by this time things has slowed down and some of the people she know had moved and Odie was now making him self distant. Angel knew what she wanted from Odie and all she was asking was that he come home and not be drunk talking crazy. She wanted to receive that same love she was given. But this was not what she was getting. But she knew her vows were for better or worse, so she thought she would pray and hang on. It was if the more she prayed the more things begin to happen. Love was in the air for Angel but there was no one to love but herself and Easton her child. She had sexual needs that needed to be met but there was know one to meet them; when she needed them met. This is where Angel would find love in her mind, what is known in the spirit ram of darkness as having a seductive spirit to invade the mind and body! At the early stage of answering the call of God; Angel would go through some things that would be dangerous; she would need to know about how the enemy would work.

Angel remember setting in the trailer house alone wanting to be love and because there was know one to answer the call she begin to find her self loving herself to satisfy the need. This immoral act would take place for about two weeks before Angel would come to her senses and discover that the enemy was using her to invade her mind and body as well as her home. There were times when she could see the shadow of the demons in the house; what had she done! Once realizing that the love she was making was not just in her mind but to a spirit of darkness. Angel want to test to see if what was happen was really happen. So they say the best way to tell if you have a bad spirit is to stand next to an animal. So one of they lady's in the trailer park Angel use to baby-sit for had a dog. So what she did was after committing an immoral act she went and stood on the porch of her house to see what reaction she would get. And in the mist of standing on the porch she looked at the dog and the dog begin to look at her and begin to go crazy as if she had done something to it. It was than that she had no dough in her mind that it was true and she had given into a seducing spirit. But Angel begins to pray, and seek God face for instruction on how to be release from the spirit. She would soon find out later on in life that she was in spiritual warfare with the enemy. She need to keep in mind that the enemy comes to steal, kills and destroy. Even in her sleep the enemy was out to get her he just did not stop there. It was here that angel would find out the enemy works in all shapes, form and fashion he have no perspective of person that he messes with except those that will not do his will. But she would learn that he even mess with the ones that are already his because he help them to cut their life span short so that they would not have a chance to submit to God. And he does this through drugs, alcohol, and lust ext. He causes one to believe that there is nothing wrong with what they are doing and by the time one realizes it he has them hook.

Angel did not know what consequences would be for her action all she know that it would take time to get these spirits out of her house and life. They just do not leave like that. Not only that she learns even though she got ride of her spirit, Odie would bring some back in the house with him UN-aware. Odie was not himself; he had got a car how Angel would never know but she would see him even less. Angel could recall the night Odie got in an accident not fare from the house; he was now gone even more but this one night as she lay awake-watching TV there was a loud crash she heard but she prayed that it wasn't Odie. So she just keep on watching TV because it was too late to be walking to see what had happen. When there was a knock at the door. It was one of the neighbors coming to tell her that it was her husband in a care accident and that know one was hurt. But the time Angel and her neighbor walked up the road to where the accident was; they had taking him to the police station. Angel made her way to the police station to find her husband because she had not giving up on him. When she arrived at the police station he was covered in blood with scares in his face, refusing to cooperate with the police.

Angel did what she could to get him to do what they were asking him so he could go home. Well he did and they went home. It seem as if the only time he really wanted to be close was when something had gone wrong for him and he needed her to be there through his pain. Angel would be there even for that if she had to because she know that the enemy was at work and he was out to get her by any means.

During this time Odie would spend time at home because they had gave him some time off because of the DUI he had received that caused the accident. Thank God that; that was the only thing they gave him.

But the only thing about him spending time at home was that he would cause more problems and sex must have been in the air and during his time off he was spending some time with some else. Angel would get the side affects of the left over from the other women. The sex demon was still in the air and it had hold of Odie and he was using it whether he knew it or not. Angel and Odie spend a week in the bed eating and sleeping and having sex. Not only that because it was at this time Odie know that he would soon have to go off in the field for some time. So he was making the best of a bad situation. During this time Odie would get to see what Angel did in her spare time. It would be at this time that Angel would find out that Odie wasn't sitting at home while she went to church on Sunday and bible class on Wednesday nights. One night while Odie was sleep she just got this strange feeling that something wasn't right, so she decided to go with her feeling she had and checked his pockets. Well to her surprise! She found out that the young lady that had been coming around selling books had all ready made her rounds. Not only was she making her rounds but also she was making them to Angel house to see Odie when she was not there. Angel could still see the look on her own face when she saw the number.

She confronted Odie about the number and he did admit that the girl had been coming around but it was not like she thought. Angel waited until she came back around to tell her what she thought and she never saw the woman again but to she don't know if Odie saw her again either and she really did not care. It was at this time she realized that Odie was still up to his old tricks of seeing other woman. It brought her to mind that she really had no regrets about something's she had done in the past. But there was still hope she thought, do not let any thing else come up or else she would have to reconsider something's.

Will it was time for Odie to go to the field for two weeks and Angel and Easton would be by their self not that Easton care he was with his friends most of the time. This would give her time to regain her self while he was gone in hopes that he would come back a better man. But only if she know what would be next. Odie had gone off to the field and it was just Angel and Easton.

It was getting cold now and it was time to feel up on the oil to keep the trailer warm. In the mean time Angel was still going to church and praying and doing all the things a wife should do. But there was this itching Angel begin to have for no apparent reason, at first she did not know what to think about the itch hoping that it would go away. Angel begin to take more baths and showers because she thought that it could just been from all the sex her and Odie were having before he left for the field. For two weeks Angel had this itch down in her vaginal area, and she was picking up weight. But what really got her the most was when one night while laying on the coach she begin to itch, but this time when she scratched some thing came off on her hand and fail on the coach. (Sitting in the smoked filled room it seems as though it was yesterday) Angel jumped to her feet and went into the bathroom and begins to see if she could see any thing. Even though she had heard of bugs that could get in the skin she had never had to experience it until now. So she went over to Cindy house and borrowed a book that would explain what Angel had. It was crabs Odie had given her before he left. She was furious with him she could not wait until he came home to comfort him about the situation. He did come home and she let him have it and all he could do was look stupid. Angel will never for get that night when she made him pick every last one off of her and for the first time she would have to shave the hair on her womb.

The worst was not over; even though the crabs where off and Odie was acting a little better but not much; at least she thought. Until Angel found out that not only had he given her crabs but also in the process she had become pregnant with his child. Angle just know that this would change Odie and he would spend more time with her and Easton because he had no father figure now consider that he was way from his real father. Odie was not seeing eye to eye even when he found out that Angel was having a baby it seem to make him no difference. Angel was so hurt that she had made up in her mind that if things continued to come up she was leaving. Little did he care because he begins to act up even more? He begins to continue to stay out even more then before. He begins to hang out with this one friend he had that was married a nice looking man. But some how seem gay. What got Angel the most that really made her make up her mind was the day when Odie came home one morning with this friend and when she woke up; there was food that had been cooked. So she asked where was hers and the rude response she got word could never replace. When he got through all Angel could do was go and sit down some where. But it was from that time she had made up her mind that she would be leaving going back home. So while he was in the street hanging out she was at home planing how to get back home and how she would do it.

This was the plan she would wait until it was pay day and she would make sure that she had a ride to the bus station and she would only take what she could and when he came home she would be gone.

But before she left, she would experience some thing she had never experience. One night while Odie was sleep the heat went off and instead of Angel trying to let Odie fix it. She decided to fix it her self. And in the mist of trying to fix it the furnace cough on fire as she ran out the house leaving Odie in the house. While standing on the outside one unreasonable though ran through her mind. Leave him in there. Knowing that was not the right thing to do; she went in the house and woke him up to get him out the house. Just to show how the enemy works; they stood there for a minute and the fire went out and Odie went in the house to make sure that every thing was okay. Even though Odie had done a lot of things in the past she could not stand there and see something happen to him after all this was still her husband for better or worst and she was beginning to believe that it was all about the worse in him.

Angel remember the dream that she had about Odie where they where fighting and his face was the face of a demon on top of her trying to kill her and all she could do was call on the name of Jesus to get him off. It was in this trailer park that Angel would experience many strange things in her life. She remember times when she could feel the forces of the enemy holding her down while she was sleep and when she tried to come out she could actually fill the evil present. Angel never told any one about the dreams or the experience she was having with spirits. But she knew that God was on her side no matter what she went through. If Angel had nothing else to hang on to she know that the word she had; and over and over she would read so that it could get in her soul; and God was teaching her; time was now drawing near and Angel would soon be leaving Odie not because she did not love him. But based on the fact that she must have married the worse of him and she was not ready to handle it. Some thing she could not deal with or at least she did not have to deal with. Angel knew she could not tell Odie she would be leaving him and she would have to leave in a discrete way. So one morning while Odie had gone off to camp or work angel had made arrangements for one of the girls in the trailer park to take her to the bus station. She had already told her mother that she would be coming back home because things where not working out. Not only that Angel know that Odie income alone could not keep them going, so the best thing to do was leave plus she could no longer starve herself or Easton trying to make ends meet. So Angel left and went back to Chicago to leave with her mother. But the enemy was not going to stop there he had plans for Angel waiting to come; only if she had of known.

CHAPTER FOUR

BRAKE AWAY

Angel moved back to her mother house and only two of her brothers where staying there now; most of them where gone, so Angel could have a room to herself as usual. Angel knew she was a strong person and independent and she knew that she would make it even with another baby on the way. Angel would now get to see her old friends again even Eric her son fathers some thing she was very happy about. Even though he was in a relationship with the woman from their pass and was about to marry her. Once Eric found out that Angel was back he came over and they talked about things that happen in their past relationship and where they might have went wrong. But they did not let that stop their friendship of caring for each other. Eric would be there for Angel the next few months until her husband would show back up.

After about four or five months has passed and Angel and Eric where spending time together; but this would soon change. On April 14, 1984, things would change for Angel and little did she know that more trouble would lie ahead. Eric was not being put back on hold. But he understood and there would always be a place in her heart for him; who know what the future would hold. Easter was the next day and even though Eric and Angel had made plans those plans would be change. There was a knock at Angel mother door and for some reason Angel know that it was bad news. She had already told Eric the bad news so that it would not be a surprise to him. Angel went to the door without opening it; she would look out the pep hole to first to see if her hunch was right and sure as it was in her mind it was Odie at the door. Angel could have just feel on the floor right there for dead. Angel opens the door only to see his face standing there. Life was some how sad for Angel again. As he entered her motherhouse with a hello; Angel response was a sad hello back and what are you doing here.

Knowing in her heart she was not happy to see him. From this point on things did not get any better. Angel did not see Eric much after Odie showed up on the scene again but she would keep in touch with him because of Easton her son who was glade to be back home with his cousins and friends also. But was even Easton getting any better did any one even stop to ask him what he was feeling or thinking about every thing that was going on. Angel knew that nothing had change with Odie and more trouble laid head. It was as if Angel could see in the future and she did not know. But all she knew was that what she saw in her mind came to pass. It was Angel and Odie again he came in a they talked and he told her that the reason why they had given him a discharge from the service; because he was having problems. Angel was not falling for anything he told her because she already knew what it was about to happen; but she married for better or worse. She was willing to go along with worse until she had enough and could not take any more. She kept telling her self; and she seems to be telling herself this a lot.

Angel stills hanging on to God and letting him handle it or lead her to handle it. Well things even started off on the wrong foot with Odie he hardly had any thing; and the things he had brought back with him; he had to put in storage all that he did not sale. As time would go on Odie did not find a job; the drinking began again along with other things. This pregnancy Angel was having this time would not be a normal one because there where to many things in the way of her having a healthy baby. She was not eating right which was the most important part of the pregnancy. Her mother who took almost any one in had a problem with the situation but refuse to say any thing until she was drinking her self. But for the love of her daughter she would have to put up with them. Odie was getting on her nerves with the drinking and staying out and do to the fact she was unhappy with this marriage.

Three months after Odie came back into Angel life it was somewhat up and down hill. The up hills where things Angel did to make her self-happy. And the downhill where things Odie did try to pull her down and she did not know if he really meant to do it. On July 15, 1984, Angel would have an early delivery this time. Stress would cause her baby to be born two months early than usual. Odie once again came in drunk and wanting to have sex. It was bad enough that he wanted to have sex too much and not even thinking about the baby. But having it any way despite what she was feeling. Angel begins to have labor pains but she was not about to go through what she went throughout the last time. This time she would make sure the baby was ready to come because of the hard labor she had before. Well considering she was only seven months it was something wrong with that picture but she was in labor. And she would have to do this one along also, because Odie was not around because he was to busy doing his on thing with women.

Angel got what she wanted this time because the next morning, which was July 16, 1984, when she got up she was claim and cool. She even took a bath and everything. She went and calls the hospital to let them know how far she was dilated and they told her to come on in. when she got there the baby head was coming out and the doctors and nurse had to push the baby head backup, because they did not know if the cored was warped around the baby neck.

Odie was not there and they had to do a C-Section on Angel. When she woke up Angel had a baby boy weighting four pounds and five ounces. This baby was little but all right. So the next morning when Odie came to the hospital to see Angel what to her surprise; Odie has suck marks on his necks. Angel just happens to be looking at his neck when she saw the marks and asked him what was wrong with his neck. Odie had brought one of his best friends out there with him, even he could not say anything. Odie could not do any thing but get up and leave. As Angel set thinking over the past tears begin to roll down her face. Where did she go wrong she asked her self as she lit up a cigarette to clam her self? What had she done to deserve this part of her life she would never understand and only God known? Angel will never for get that night for the sample reason her temperature went up and the doctors thought something was wrong with the surgery so they begin to start examining her. Angel laid there and started crying she want to tell them that nothing was wrong with her and it was only do to her husband that her temperature was up. What could she do about the situation at hand? Nothing! When Angel went home the baby did not come with her based on the fact that the baby had to gain a few more pounds before they would let him come home. At first Angel was heart broken to the point she had a set back. But she would have to take care of herself for the baby sake.

Now that Angel had two kids it was time for Angel to start looking for a place even with the welfare check she was getting; she would soon have to leave her mother house because Odie wasn't getting any better and she needed a place to feel free, not to be a burden on her mother. But during this time Odie would go through some things that would let Angel know that she was right again another women in the picture. Winter had se in and Angel had found a place but could not move in until she had come up with all the money to move in with. In the mean time Odie was having an affair with his ex-girlfriend. Well one night Angel got a call from the hospital telling her to come to the hospital because her husband had gotten shot. When she heard the words shot her heart fail. So she went to see what was going on and hope that he wasn't dead or any thing. When she arrived at the hospital she found home lying on the table with a gunshot wound in his hand. So she did what most wives would do and that was to find out what happen. He told her that he had been in a lounge with his ex-girlfriend and some one shot through the place and he got one of the bullets. How much more did she have to take she begin to ask her self.

Angel did found an apartment down stairs from her sister in-law and brother in the building they there where living in that her father and mother had owned and they decided to let them have the apartment; it was a nice one bedroom and it would have to do for now. But little did Angel know some of the thing she would have to go through while leaving in this apartment. Angel still had God in her life and any or everything she went through she know that God was standing by her side even when she felt as though she could not take any more.

Angel begin to do things for her self she knew what she wanted out of life and she got a job to make ends met and help pay bills. Angel had very little all her life but she was not settling for it. Proverty was not one of the things she wanted in life and she had gone without most of her life growing up. Angel knew that it would take some schooling and degrees to get what she wanted. So she went and worked what jobs she could and went to school and got a degree as a typist. But many other things would happen in the course of two years in this apartment. Angel would have many trials she would have to face with Odie along with the drinking and drug demon he was carrying. So many things happen while living in the apartment Angel did not know if she wanted to go back and recall these things that happen.

To start off with she recall times when Odie stayed out and did not come home. That she did not mind. But then there came the times when he was working and messing around the corner with another women and took this woman out of town in their new care and had the nerve to call her from the people house. Even though Odie was doing a lot of things Angel did not find it in her heart to give back what she was getting. She would take it to God in pray. Angel knew more about the word and how to use it. So when she wasn't letting herself get the best of her she would leave the matter alone. But then there were times when she had to say or do something. A little while after they move in Angel begin to have trouble with Odie because he wanted to fight her for his troubles. Angel remember the time when she was working a Wallgo supermarket and Odie was watching Easton one night and he was drinking and cause the car to almost crash on the highway was Easton ran to his father house which was not far and told his father what had happen. Eric was mad and called Angel by this time now Eric had gotten married to the women he had brought to her house. But she loved Easton as if he was her own. Once she got the call she was ready to leave work and when she got out side Odie was standing outside high wanting for her to give her his side of the story. Well Angel did not know what to do; so they went home and then because she could not drive, he had to take her over to Eric motherhouse to pick Easton up. When they arrived Eric was sitting on the porch waiting for Angel. Thank God she thought Easton was okay but Eric wanted to take him to the hospital to have him check out and Angel agreed. On the way out of Eric House Odie said something smart that Eric did not like. Now need she remind you that Eric was his short man five feet in height and Odie was this tell man about six feet, but Eric was the type of man that nothing made him any difference and he was not scared of any thing.

While Odie was making his smart commits Eric was getting even madder, so while Eric family and my self was trying to keep him calm Odie was not making matters better with his drunken talk. So before she knew it Eric had got up and went in the street where Odie was and started beating him up. she tried to stop Eric from beating Odie and he did but this would be the best five-minute beating Odie ever have. Deep down inside she wanted to laugh so badly but she had to wait until the time was right. The next morning when Odie woke up his eye was big and swollen. Then he wanted to take it out on her but she was not having it; he got what he deserved. She could also remember the time when t was close to Christmas and Easton father brought him a piano like toy that cost. So Eric gave it to Angel to bring home because he know how Odie was. So Angel brought the gift home and when Odie saw that Eric had brought it he tour it up and what did he do that for. Angel was given Easton a sign to leave the house and go to is father house; but telling him to go and take the trash out; and he did; he went to his father house once again and told him what had happen. So by this time Angel know that she would leave the house also, and she did; taking off to her sister house but leaving the baby in the house with him.

Angel called Eric upon arriving at her sister house telling him what had happen. Then a little while later Eric and his wife and Easton came where she was.

She realizes that she had left the baby with him and called the police to met her at the house so that she could get her baby. When they arrived at the house he was still there was blood on his clothes. Little did she know that Eric had; been to the house already and beat him up again. So the police came and told him to give her the child and he did. While Eric was sitting across the street in his car.

Odie tried to get her to stay but she was not having it. Angel know that if she stayed there with him things wasn't going to be right so she just went back to her sister house and spent the night, this would not be the end of what was about to happen. Angel still remember the time when one night Odie and her brother had come into the house to try and get some money out of her to buy drugs. Angel was that the stove and Odie still had gual on his finger from when he had gotten his finger shot off. So while standing at the stove he asked her for some money and when she would not give him any he took off his Gaul and wrap it around her neck choking her. It was nothing she could do but hope that God was on her side. After he let her go she was just amazed at what had just took place and her brother was sitting in the front room and had not heard a thing. How much more did she have to take. Well he did not just stop there she could even remember the time where the more she got out and tried to work to make things happen; the more he did things to try to bring her down.

Odie was now on drugs with the help of her brothers who was apart of making that happen. Some time later Odie obtained a job but would not be able to keep it long. After about six months Odie lost it because of the drugs. He did not know angel knew but she did. As well as the woman he was messing around with around the corner because her twin told her. Angel was still going to God and still reading the word trying to do the right things. Not to say that she was still human and she made mistakes. But not like the mistakes Odie was making. Angel was being psychically and mentally being abused by Odie. She could remember the time when she started leaving him. One time she left and went and spent the night over to her motherhouse just to see what kind of reaction he would give knowing he was messing around. So she did go and spend the night and he came the next day talking crazy to her. Well on their way home because they did not have a car at this time they had to get on the bus. Then bus fare was cheap; but while they where riding the bus he called her every thing in the book because for once she was out and not him. Angel had never been so embarrassed in her life to be called all kinds of names by the man she vows to death do us part. And it did not stop there even when they got home things got worse. He told her he was going to treat her like a hoe! And he took what he wanted and then spit on her leaving her there. Angel was so out done until she just did not know what to do; but to get up and go and wash her self off. The only person she could think of that had gotten spit on was Jesus, so to keep from doing something stupid she just considered her self to be blessed. So that next day Angel went to her grandmother because she was close to her; told her the story of what happen and she will never forget the worse her grandmother told her. If he had of spit on me he would not live to tell any one about it.

He did not stop there she could remember the time when he pushed her through their front room window; while a other people where standing on the porch because he was mad. He did not even stop there she could remember the time when he put a knife to her neck and told her he would kill her and for no reason. How much more could she take; all she was asking for was a husband she could love and he love her back. Was that asking too much! Angel was growing tried of the physical and mental abuse. It was after the knife to her neck matter that struck something in her as to say that she was not going to take any more because this was not God will for her life. Well the next day Angel asked God if Odie would just come in; in peace the next day things could be all right. The next day came and Angel tried to go about the day as usual with work and coming home reading the word. But Odie came home that night but he was not in good mud and he was drunk. He came in the house and for no apparent reason just started cursing and talking to her any kind of way. Angel will never for get that night she just set there because she smoked at the time and she had not had a cigarette all day and her he come with the bull she said in her mind. So when he got through cursing and things Angel asked him if he had a cigarette and he said no; she asked him if he had any money to buy any and he said no. Then he went into the bedroom andlay down and went to sleep. For about two hours Angel set there trying to figure out what was that about and what had she done for the way he came in.

Well after sitting and thinking and wishing she had a cigarette to help calm her nerves she found none. But by this time other things begin to inflate her mind. Revenge sat in the more she sat there it seems as though something was taking over her. Angel tried to clam herself and tell her self that revenge belong to God; to this voice of reasoning she know revenge belong to God so it will be up to him to stop what she was about to do. Angel begins to put a pot on the stove with grease in it and then she turn the fire on it. Angel went back and sat in the same spit she was when he first entered the door reading her bible. Angel began to ask the Lord what had she done wrong to deserve this kind of treatment. All she had been doing for the past seven years was trying to be a good wife and serve God was that asking too much. There where times in angel life when she could have probably had a better life because she had many offers from other guys she knew that really cared for her but she would refuse because she believed that marriage was right. But now she know that some time we can marry but if he was not Godly/ or God had not sent him he was not the right one; and she was begining to see it now.

Well angel begin to pray to the Lord and tell him that if what she was about to do was not his will then he needed to stop her. God must not have heard her pray because Angel found her self going outside to pull the car in the alley, and putting Odie Jr. in the care and then putting some clothes in the car. Lord know what was about to come next; angel found herself going to the stove and one last time asking God to stop her because this was not his will but the work of the enemy. Again God did not get the prayer because angel got the pot off the stove that had been on all this time; and proceeded to the bedroom door and she as she stood there looking upon Odie sleep all she cold see was the things he had done. It was then that she would throw the grease and she could just see the grease go up in the air and down on him. In the blink of and eye Angel was out thedoor and in her car with Odie Jr. by the time she reach the car all she heard was a loud scream, that was so loud until even the baby had to ask if that was a ghost and angel reply was yes and drove off. Angel know that this was not her but what every it was had taking control. So she and Odie Jr. drove 176 miles to Rock Island where she know they would be safe. And Rock Island was where her grandmother lived now.

But the whole time she was on the road she talk with God all the way there. So she know God had control of the care because she reason with God all the way there. Once she made it there she told her grandmother what had happen and then she went in the basement to weep sorely.

Angel will again never for get the words of her grandmother; she told her to get up and come out of that basement because she had done nothing wrong god know what he had done to her. But that was not comforting to Angel she need God to forgive her for what she had done.

In a couple of days Angel would be able to let it pass a little but the thoughts would always be there no matter what. Then she just knew things would never be the same between them. Odie would be scared for the rest of his life and every time he looked at him self in the mirror he would think of her for a long time. These and other thoughts cross Angel mind; even the thought of will she be able to go back; only time would tell.

Yes! Time would tell after about a mouth in Rock Island of Sleeping on the floor Angel would and could go back. After all Odie had forgiven her and wanted her to come back home and still be with her. He explains to her that he knows that it was his fought that it happen. A lot of things cross Angel mind; she did not know his real reason for wanting her back home. What if he tried to do the same thing to her one-day? But like most wives that are blinded Angel returned to Chicago back to Odie and the house. Angel know that things could never be the same but she hoped that this would make him think before he react. Odie never really physically abused angel any more but he would emotionally abuse her based on the fact he did not know what would happen if he had put his hands on her again. Angel went back to going to church; which was around the corner from her house. Original Holy Antioch Baptist church. Where some of her family members went. And even found a job to help catch up on the bills because what she did causes them to fall behind in bills. So angel got a job and begins to work while Odie stayed at home and was suppose to watching the kids.

Angel would soon find out that nothing but a little bite had change. He begins to do drugs heavy and even begin to bring it into the house around the kids. Angel could remember coming home not knowing what to expect. Until one day she came home and found Odie and some women in her house getting high. This was enough for angel she could not take any more; so in the mist of Odie talking to her at the car; Odie walked off to go to the store and in the mist of him walking off Angel drove off with the thought that she was not coming back. There was nothing else she could do he had to help him self. With the fact that he had wanted to get help because he was not just destroying him self; but her and the kids. By this time Easton had no respect for him and the way he was doing him neither would he in the future.

Angel left and went and stayed with her mother again' it was the only pace Angel know that there would be a place for her even if it were on the floor. Things would be okay for Odie for a little while he would pack up every thing and put in storage and go back to leaving with his aunt. In the mean while angel mother friend was moving out of her apartment and told angel she could move in so long as she paid the rent and did not cause any trouble for her because the place would still be in her name. Angel agreed to do so. Trouble did not stop there for angel; she still had to deal with Odie because he had no transportation and he would be coming for the car.

One night while angel slept with her mother just before it was time for her to get up for work. Angel mother called to her and told her to get up because her car was on fire. Angel replied was mother it is to early in the morning to be playing; girl your car is on fire she replied again. When angel got up to look out the window it was true. Angel car was on fire and people where standing outside looking at it. The car was totaled there was very little left because they just don't make cars like they use to. Angel was sure it was Odie because he had called the day before asking her for the car and she would not give it to him; not to mention the time before; and he call that morning to ask her how was things going. Angel wasn't going to let that stop her; she would have to trouble getting to work but this was not going to make her get back with him not even for the worse she was tried and ready to move on.

Angel was able to pay the car off with what the insurance gave her but they would not give her another one.

It was at this time angel would take the offer that her mother friend had given her; so she move in and things where going okay. At the end of eight nine, things begin to turn for the worse again for angel to start off her father illness would soon come. Her and her twin brother Bobby would attend the funeral it would be the dead of winter and angel would have to drag the kids out in the could to the funeral. Upon attending the funeral she would go through a thing because he was now gone. She even felt guilty about not going to get a place for them to live together; as he wanted; guilt would eat at her. Angel father had been asking her for some time to get a place that was big enough so they could live together. For some strange reason angel father after all these years now wanted to live with her. Angel felt as if her father was only doing this because he no longer wanted to stay with the women he had been living with for a great number of years. So she never got the place he kept asking for. Angel found out that she was not as strong as she thought she was. He was dressed in a three peace brown suite with the hat to go with it; and the caste match. When angel saw him she broke down in tears and asking God to forgive her because she did not fore fill her father request, but it was to late there was nothing she could do now but receive what God had done.

She would remember some the times she spent with her father. He would come around from time to time to visit her and her mother. They're where time s when she would go to his house to visit him before he got sick. He was a drinker and nothing or no one could stand in the way of that. Angel did not care about whether he gave her money or anything like that she just wanted to be around her father for who he was. She would in the future find her self-living around the same area he once lived. Memories! It would take angel some time to get over the fact that her father was gone but she would all ways keep him in her memories of her mind. She would discover that people never really die; because they are always on /or in your memories as if they where still here.

Life had to go on for angel she continued to talk with God. At this time Odie had not completely giving up and he would come around every now and then when he had no where else to go and angel would let him in. This would go on for some time because angel was still working even though she was on the bus and from time to time one of the girls would bring her home.

Even though angel had a place to stay now; Odie was still up to his old tricks when angel was out at work Odie was out playing and getting high. Little did he know that his luck would soon run out and the jail had a cell waiting for him? Summer of 90, had come and angel had now stop working and was drawing unemployment because the job she was working went out of business; so she could still pay her bills.

Considering that Odie was still in the picture with angel and still doing the same thing but only this time he would get him self into some thing that the could not get out of. About the month after angel had stop working some thing had took place with Odie and angel twin brother kids mother because she got high to. Angel had no knowledge of what had taking place. So through the help of her brother angel would find out the Debbie had filed child molestation charges against him. So one day while angel and Odie was sitting in the house watching TV there was a knock at the door and Angel started for the door Odie went and stood in the kitchen as to try and hide himself; while angel proceeded to the door.

When she looked out the key hold she saw a man and a women detective standing outside the door. Angel knows that they were about to do. So she opens the door and pointed to the place where he was standing and they proceeded to go and get him. He had the funniest look on his face as to say you told them where I was. And she had the look on her face to say you made your bed now lay in it. Then they hand cuff him and took him out the door. Angel was now free from a mental and physical abuse marriage. God had answered a prayer Odie was now about to drown in his dirty work he had done.

Other thing would happen now that Odie was out the way. Angel oldest son was now in an environment would cause him to doing things she had know ideal. She found out that he was not going to school, and he was now in a gang activity. She did what she could to try and talk to him about what he was doing but it did not help. So he would have to find life out the hard way. She often felt she did not pay enough attention to him, as she should have; but it was too late, but what appeared to be heaven would now turn to hell.

CHAPTER FIVE

FINAL CALL

Angel was now free even though she did not completely for get Odie after all she was still married to him. She would go to see him on his visiting day and take Odie Jr. out there with her. It was during this time angel thought she could get her self together. Angel would spend the next six months trying to pull her life together. During this time angel spent most of her time going to church and trying to do what was right by herself and her kids. In between this time angle had no one in her life. She met this guy that use to visited his mother and father down the street; his name was Sean. At this point in angle life she did not trust any man and it seem as if every one that she would met had a problem. Angel was kind hearted she allowed Sean to come over just to see what he was about and to see how things would go. She really knew from the beginning now where because he was married. She still remember him he was tall dark and somewhat handsome. But the man had some strange qualities about his self; even thought he worked Sean had a wife some thing angel was not for. She was not a custom to taking another woman husband even though some of them that she met were married angel could not see herself with another woman husband. Beside Sean was strange when angel would let him come over to see her he would always bring a six pack of beer in a bag that he carried ever where he went. She often wonders if he had some thing in there to kill some one with in there. He was always telling Angel that she had never had a real organism and the he could make her toes stand up if she would just give him the chance. Angel never gave him the chance even thought it all sounds tempting.

But little did he know or did angel know that the Lord would call him home soon. Angel thought Sean could be a nice person even though he was cheap and never gave or brought her anything the whole time he would come to see her not even a pop. Was it that serious angel thought; this man wanted to have sex but angel know that would never happen. Angel saw Sean for about three months then she decided that she would stop seeing him because she did not want to get his hopes up high. He wasn't to thrill and he even wanted to get a little angry.

But what could he do he was married; but little did angel no what was up the road for either of them. About six months of living alone angel would allow room the enemy to come into her life again but only this time it would be a little worse then before.

Sean did die a little while after angel stop seeing him and she could not believe it when she heard the news. She would still go and see Odie in jail because they had given him a few years in jail. So she did not have to worry about him. In the mean time angel would go to her mother house and spend time over there; and in the middle of being over there one day her baby brother had a friend of his over there and from time to time when she looked in the room where they was he was looking at her as if to say I would like to get to know you. Need angel remind herself that her brother was only twenty-five years at old so his friend could not have been that much older? Angel really never gave him any though until one day when she was hanging out the window one day over there.

Angel was the type of women that know what she wanted in a man and most of the men she met just would not do. Some how she still felt in her heart that Eric still would have been the one for her. And she knew that she would not find any one else like him.

During this time angel collected this thought about the past and the future, she was now out of work. Based on the fact she knew that she did not want to work any more slave labor job, so she would take this time out to find a better paying job. And this would give her time to find out where he might have went wrong in her life. And why up until this point in her life had been so dim. It could have been something wrong with her instead of them, but what?

Could it be that she was looking for men in all the wrong places or could it have been that she was not suppose to be with a man until God showed her, only the future knew.

So she would spend the next six months trying to find her self and make a better future for her.

Angel continued to travel in between the past and the present to see what she could find out that would help her to better understand what was going on in her life. She begin to reflect back on things that happened after she stop seeing Sean. Angel life would turn for the worse based on the fact that after she just had got out of a friendship; she would find her self into something else. Angel would now go and get her self into another relationship that would not be easy to get out of.

Angel went back to remembering her brother friend and how they first met. As angel recalled the day she was standing in the hallway of her mother house looking out the window when the voice say; you should not be hanging out the window like that; it was this same young men that was looking at her in her brothers room; but only this time he was looking up her dress from behind her coming up the stairs. Angel realized what he was talking about she proceeded to let him know that he should not be looking at women in that way. Angel never really gave him another thought but what he said she did and that was to get out the window. After having that small conversation with him it would be sometime later he would invite himself to her house for dinner. As she remember it just happen one day when she was in her window talking to some one; he asked the question 'when can I come to dinner? Angel replied never but he would show up one day when she had fix dinner. Angel would never for get the way Larry looked when she first met him. He was built and had a jerry curl in his head and far skin nice looking young man angel thought. When do you want me to come Larry replied! Angel sating I will let you know. It would be about two months later or so when there was a knock at the door. Angel need to remind her self may be the Lord was sending her someone to be with; so she thought at that time.

She was about to get the shock of her life. Thinking back angel would advice any one to be careful what you ask God for. Angel remembers what she asked God for one night when she felt lonely and had known one to talk to. She remembers asking god to send her some one that loves her. Well some how she was not pacific enough because what she was about to get words for her would not be able to describe.

Angel will never for get the day when Larry showed up at her house for dinner. She had cook some macaroni and cheese and chicken ext. and he ate and from that day he was coming around. She still remembered some of the things he told her while sitting at her kitchen table and eating her food. Larry explained that the young woman he was now with had done him wrong and she had her family after him and he had done every thing he could for her as she went out cheating on him and just a whole lot of things. Angel like a dummy believed some of what Larry was telling her because she to was in a bad relationship; but no one in their right mind should have been able to see the signs of what she just had been through. Signs that should have told her that; this are what he was putting her through (the other woman I mean). As angel begin to look back she could see all the signs God had given her, but yet it was as if she had know control over what was happen. There where times when she had control and yet she did not take them and when she did take them, she found herself right back in the same boat.

The relationship was off the ground now angel and Larry were now going together; God was given angel sign, but what happen.

When angel and Larry first started out it was nothing but lies from the jump. At the beginning of the relationship; Larry was gone for about two weeks and when he return he told her that his ex-girlfriend had put the police on him and had him locked up. Angel thought okay. But angel was allowed to return to work but only she would be on the bus now. Winter was now setting in the year of 89, angel was not working now and there would be time when some more money was coming in would do just find. So angel decided to rent her nephew a room for a few dollars a week.

In renting this room angel told her nephew that he was to have no drugs what so ever in the house because she was not going to have the law coming in her house and yet he agreed. So some time had gone by so one day while angel and Larry was in the house her nephew Ben cam e in the house he and another friend. So they went into the room as usual, they stayed for about thirty minutes then they left. After about ten minutes had passed angel youngest brother came to her house and told her that the police had Ben and his friend down stairs searching them. In and instant angel got nervous and did not know what to do. But she was hoping that he had kept his promise he had made her, so she put the lock on the door just in case. A little while later the door opens it was the police asking her to open the door. Angel did after the fact that they had; the key to open themselves.

Angel open the door and the office pulled out a piece of paper stating something Angel to this day still do not know what the paper read. So she let them in and they pushed her nephew in on the floor and his friend. They were black of course and they begin to search the house with Angel permission. Angel could remember that night well after she gave the permission that's was all they needed. They went throughout the house and tour up ever thing they could that was not nailed down. Then it was time to go into the room where the broken promise would be found. In this room there was a waterbed and a nineteen-inch TV. After entering the room they begin to search the room and in the mist of searching one officer went to the TV and begin to search behind it and under it and came out with a brown jar with some content of white power ball. Then he came out with a knot of money. Angel could not do anything but stand there and look. She was disappointed with her nephew. They begin to ask her question and then they went in the front room where he was and begin to ask him question about who stuff was it and he answered that it belong to him. They pick him up off the floor and took down the stairs. One of the officers talked with Angel and she told them that she had asked him not to bring any thing in the house and he did not respect it. This was the result of what could happen when he did. After the arrest was made and they had taking her nephew down stairs one of the officer took the five hundred dollars and gave it to her. By now Larry was staying with Angel and this night she found her self standing for some one she knows nothing about which was

Larry. The police was about to arrest him also until Angel spoke up. From this night on Angel would not go through this again. She would know her rights and what could and should not happen. She would go back to school for law.

There would be a time when Larry would ask Angel to go to court with him because he claim that this ex-girlfriend was taking him to court because he jumped her. So angel went to court and he won the case. It would be here that Angel would take care of him. What was she thinking?

Angel was beginning to make a fool of her self even more, it was as if she was not getting wiser but dumber and dumber.

There where times when she would walk with him over to his mother house and the route they would take they would have to pass his ex-girlfriend house. Never thinking that he was going this way to see if he could see her coming in or out of her house. Larry knew every one in the neighborhood. But little did she know that he had just about all the women in the neighborhood, but she would not discover this until it was too late.

There would be times when Angel would except calls from Odie because he was still locked up, but she was living a lie. She would tell Odie that she was not seeing any one, when all the time she had Larry sitting in the next room, and telling him that she know longer want him. Which was the truth but Larry would not want to hear that.

So they would begin to get into it. But not until she would find out one day when her cousin came over to discover that he had went with her cousin some years back. Angel could not believer what he was telling her, but she still did not have sense enough to get out. Housing would soon find out about the incident that happen and would ask her to move out of the apartment.

After this event was over Angel would have to move and this to where she would find out the real deal about Larry. Angel would also learn that a person would have to be careful what you ask God for because he will send just what you ask him for. Angel would soon move back into her motherhouse but would let Larry talk her into going to his motherhouse to stay. Upon going to Larry motherhouse to stay; she would find out that this would be the worse thing she could have ever done. Here she was leaving her children in one place while she stay some where else again for a relationship.

But where else could she go. She could continue to stay with her mother and sleep on the floor, but that floor would get hard some times. No Angel through so she would leave the kids at her motherhouse and spend most of her nights over to Larry motherhouse and just pays her way. Larry stayed in the projects on the seventh floor. And the look of this apartment was a mess with mice every where.

After about a couple of months into the relationship Angel begin to see what she had gotten her self into was a mistakes and all the signs where there. Angel could remember the first time Larry had put his hand on her. The worse would now show up about Larry. They where on there way back to Larry mother house and this night he was mad because she was now doing things he did not like. She was still talking to her husband, when he felt it should be over with by now, but Angel was still given him support.

While they were walking down the streets and just when they got close to his motherhouse they were arguing about her not wanting to stay with him and he pushed her across the streets. Angel could feel that there was something wrong and that this relationship would not be a good one. The way Larry would like to have sex with Angel was a sign when she stops to think about it. When a man is willing to do any thing to a woman that he hardly knew her some thing is wrong and he is looking for a strong commit between to two of them. So women be careful whom you give your body to. The bible says that your body is the temple that House the Holy Spirit. And the devil would love to destroy it. It would not only be that but there will be soul ties included. And once this happen there is a big price to pay to get out of it.

Angel was now in a relationship and God was about to prepare her for some things she could not handle. It started off as a slow abuse there where times when Angel had know freedom and every where she went Larry was sure to go. Angel was not use to every time she moved he moved to. Angel could remember the night when she just know that she would not make it through the night because what had happen to her by Larry. It was in the month of September, one night when her husband had called from jail and wanted to talk to her and Larry was there. Angel just thought that he would get over it but Larry had just a little more then getting over it in mind. Angel know some thing was wrong but instead of following her first mind she did the opposite when they say follow your first mind it is true as she would find out.

Angel was not lost in thought of traveling back in time it was as if she was desperate to find out. She was asking God to show her all the mistakes she had made not to dwell on the past but gain wisdom after what she had been through. That night angel got in the car with Larry, because at this time Angel had her nephew keep the car while he was in jail he told her to keep until he got out and she did. And as she begins to drive he begins to question her about talking to Odie on the phone. Angel did not know what to say because she had made a statement that Larry took serious. He wanted her to stop talking to him on the phone. Well that night would be the beginning of the end of what she thought she had got away from and that was abuse.

He begin to hit Angel as she continued to drive Angel was not use to be attacked in a car so fear set in. When he asked her a question that she could not explain he would he her again with his fist. Then he made her drive to the lake and told her to get out the car. One thing angel was not crazy enough to get out the car. So he hit her again and told her to get out the car. But after so many hit she begin to fight back; if she were going to die she would be trying to fight back.

Once he saw that she was trying to fight back he pulled out a knife on her and told her he would kill her. Angel was really scared at this point and did not know what to do. Even though she had not known this man a couple of months what had she got her self into? Well she would make it through the night but this would be one long night to remember. Angel knows that he was not letting her go anywhere, but she did want him to stop hitting her. He made her drive to the lake because he was going to kill her and drop her in the lake, but God know that Angel might have been a fool but not that big of a fool and he had angels watching over her for ever mistake she made. Angel got a few more licks once they arrive at the lake and there was even a time when she wanted to run him over because he got out the car and told her to get out.

Because Angel was not a killer she did not have the guts to do it. She just set in the car and did not open the door for him until he decide to get back in the car and go to his mother house. Even when they had arrived at his motherhouse she still had the arge to still run him over but he waited until she got out the car first. Larry did not stop there once he got upstairs in his motherhouse he begins to hit her again and she would hit him back. Angel just knows that her face would be bruised that next morning and her family would be able to see what was going on. It appears that death was around Angel and she would feel it present. That entire night angel could not sleep thinking about what she needed to do. To get out this mess she had gotten her self into. She thought about jumping out the seven-floor window but she was not trying to kill her self. She just wanted to get away from him that night. She did not have enough sense to tell him to let her out because she did not know what he would do.

His mother locked the bars up at night. But she stayed even though she could not wait until morning.

Angel would get through a lot before this so call relationship would have its end. She would have to go throw many more fights, arguments, being accused, and everything else. This is where angel would find her strengths and weakness and this would not take a week or months but this would take years. If frighten her just to think about all those years. But she must say you live and learn. Learning is what she would be doing; she know s she had went through some things with her husband and yet he would put her through some thing that she hoped and prayed that she would live to tell about. What she was about to put her self through would be more than just a testimony.

For the married and the single women. Through it all; she could do was say to her self was that this was only a test and that God was going to bring her out. God had something he wanted her to do and he was trying to get her attention and believer her he had it.

The man she had allowed in her life had about two personalities, with who know how many spirits, he was a liar, thief, and what every else one could think of. And she do not to this day believe he know who he was. She say this because when she begin to go back in the past he said that he was dead and they brought him back to life when he was locked up in prison. This man lied about his age Angel did not know for sure how old he was because when she mate him he told her that he was twenty-five. The enemy just had him and even he knows it. Because all he would say is that he asked the Lord to let him die with his worldly people; what ever that meant. Getting away would not be easy.

So the next day arrived finally Angel was glade to see day light which meant that she could now make her way to her mother house and get away for Larry. Not only that she was not sure if she would tell her family what had happen the night before. When she arrived at her motherhouse and he was sure to follow her there. Larry was also a stalker little did Angel know but she would soon find out. Well after the day was over with it was time he thought to go to his motherhouse, but little did he know that this was not her plan. She was not going home with him now or any other night.

So when he came and told her he was ready to go he took her down stairs and in a treating way told her he was ready to go and when she try to refused he told her that yes she was going. So when Angel went back up the stairs she told her mother that he was trying to force her to go home with him and she did not want to go. So just before she could get threw telling them there was a knock at the door it was him asking her what was taking her so long. That is when she told him that she was not going with him. He begins to call her in the hallway Angel refuses because she knew what she was up against. She had some ideal of what she had got her self into, but the problem was now how she would get out. If was as if she would see the devil in human form there is know other way she could put it. As she continued to remember tears begin to come into her eyes.

Will she was free that night because her mother called the police and Larry took off and Angel brother came to get her and took her some where else. Angel would go to her sister house first for a night then she would go to her brother house for a week because they where going out of town and need some one to watch their house until they got back so she went over there for a week but only to find out that her troubles had just begun. By the end of the week of staying at her brother house; Larry would have gotten the number from her other brother Keith and was calling her to find out what she was doing. And to let her know that he was not going to stop there.

When angel arrived at her sister house which would be the next stop this is when she would find out that he was stalking her and how could he be in so many places at one time.

Angel was on her way to the store when she had not been at her sister house that long. That's when she was on her way; she could feel his presents in the air as if she was being followed and when she turned around to look back there he was behind her. Some fear came over her but she could not show how much she was afraid of him. Angel knew that this was too much power for one person to have over another and some thing was wrong. It was if a spell had been place on her; every thing he did or said Angel would pick up with it or go along on it. At this time he was not doing any thing for angel. She would live with her sister until she could afford her own place. Well he followed her to the store and back and she had him to come through the back of the fence so that her sister could not see him; he would not leave until he got what he wanted.

Larry keep coming over and she could still remember the day when he came over and they had a argument and he would pinch Angel and leave a mark on her. She would be sure not to go places with him because she did not know what he was capable of doing to her. Well angel was saving some of her money so she could get her own place because she know that Larry was causing problems not just for her but for other people including her family. That same day angel was afraid to tell Larry she did not want him. So she allowed him to continue to come around her even though it was not what she wanted, but she know that he was not about to leave (what was Angel problem was there was some kind of spell put on her or was she just stupid). Angel was back with him falling for his lies, fear, anger, jealousy, accusing he used it against her. To get what he wanted done. But it was at this point it was God allowing Angel to see in the future some of the things that would happen to her. Her gifts were in operation; and it was not looking too good for her.

Angel got the apartment next door from her sister; it was a one bedroom. It wasn't what she wanted but it would have to do for now. The only thing she was not please with was that She knew that Larry was taking her kindness for a weakness. She knew Angel move in she went and got the things she had stored and she went and got her a new bed. He begins to move his things in she know this only meant trouble. Once she was settle in she decided that she would try to do some things for her self and her kids. So she continued to work at Spiegel until she got laid off. But in between time many things would happen; some things she would have to ask God about on how to deal with him with his guide.

As angel sat back remembering not to the fact to be hurt and angry; but to see where she had gone wrong and what could she do to make her life right. She knows that Larry was taking her kindness for a weakness. She knows that he was a great pretender and if it did not take much to make him angry. He did have a problem beating up on woman and she had experience this with her own eyes one night; when some of her family friends was fighting and we just happen to be walking up; so once he found out what was going on he walked up to the girl and just started beating her in the face with his fist. Angel had never seen any thing like it before. Expect with what he had done to her. Larry also was one of those kind of guys that it was okay if he talked to woman new or old; but the person that was going with him better not try to talk to any one she use to go with or knew.

Angel would take much abuse from Larry during her stay in this apartment; but by the grace of God she would make it through this and other test and trials. But as the bible say they only come to make you strong. During angel stay at this home some things; she would learn some things of how the enemy will work to steal, kill and destroy a person if they are not strong enough. It was during this time that Angel would learn the real deal of what it was to stalk, having some one around twenty four hours a day. During this time Angel would in the mist make and set goals for her self she want to go back to school and work to make ends meet again. Not only that she had two sons she had to look out for.

Angel remembers the time when she was working at spiegals outlet store; Larry was not working and had not worked sense the first time she met him. But they're where times when she would work and extra hour or two for more money. Angel knows that she would have trouble on her hand if she stayed over with out letting him know; but that was a chance she would have to take. She still remember the day when she stayed over one day and when she got off work she would go by her mother house where he would be sitting waiting for her. When she got half way to her motherhouse there he was waiting in between the building of the projects waiting for her to see if she had been with any one. Fear was set all over her because she did not know what he would do. So he begin to question her about why she was late getting home and the more she tried to explain he begin to get angry. And hit her and push her and he even told her that she was not going to her motherhouse to check on her son. But she was not hearing it.

Larry was the kind of guy that he could do what ever he wanted and say what ever he wanted; but she better not try it. Angel could still feel the fear she felt all those year s she was with Larry. But even though she was afraid she was not letting go of God or his word but she had messed up and it was going to take a miracle to get her out. Angel tried to remember some good times that she might have had with Larry but there where not many. She could remember the time when she first met him, but the rest of the time would be down hill. Larry would go out and stay our for as long as he wanted and angel did or said nothing. He would go to other woman house and sit and talk about her like a dog and it they made him mad he would come home and take it out on her. Angel could remember the time when she was forced to have sex out of fear of what he would do if she refused.

Angel could remember one time when her and Larry and one of his cousins went to the mall and because he was mad with her and because he was trying to impress them; he went and set at another table with another woman and started talking to her right in front of her face. She had never been so humiliated in her life. But when she got home they had a few worked and they begin even struggle just to let him know that he wasn't know body. She would remember the time when Larry brought this skinny dark girl to her house and told her that she was his half sister and with angel not knowing she believed it; but only to find out some time later that this woman he had been bringing to her house was some one he had been going with. She still could remember he even asked her for money for this woman and she was doing drugs.

Living in this apartment would be times when angel get tried and tried to do some thing about what was being done to her. At this time she was staying next door to her sister and nephews so at least she had some kind of back up; and she would have to use what she had. She remember her first black eye; after going through some hard times with Larry; angel had got tried of begin missed treated and she know that this was not be east thing for him and he was not going to take it easy even after all the things he had done to her. Even though her ex-husband was getting out of jail and this could mean that he would be out the picture.

Angel know that she was not going to take her ex-husband back because he was insecure and use to having a roof over his head by women she was still in for a ruff ride. Well one day in the summer of ninety when angel finally got the nerve to put him with the help of her older son and nephews because even they where tried of the way he was treating her. Taking advantage of her and abusing her; he got up in the middle of the night during and argument they where having and told Larry to leave and if he did not leave he would have to answer to him. Now Eric Jr. was a four feet and two inch person but had no remorse about what he did or said. Because the streets life had mad him a little monster. Will after seeing that he could have trouble on his hands he left but he did not go far. Larry had got in real good with the girl upstairs; so he could go up there and keep and eye on her at the same time. It was at this time angel and Larry had a car that they both put money into but he would wind up with the car.

So one day when Larry came by concerning her ex-husband who was not out. Angel had this strange feeling that some thing was going to happen. Angel was still going to church that she was not going to give up on no matter what happened. Angel well never forget that day; she had just came back from walking her youngest son to school and went in the house and laid down when there was a knock at the door. She knows that it was Larry and he was not coming for anything. It was here at this time that angel discovered that had a gift that was in operation and that was she was able to see thing happen before they happen; and it would be at this time God would show her what Larry was going to do. So she got up and let him in when her first mind told her not to; she would learn that what it really meant to follow the firs mind. Angel and the girl next door had become friends because she was going through some things with the guy she was living with also; but it was nothing like what angel was going through. It would be here that she would introduce angel to a new church home. The same one that she was going to and angel would grow even more.

So he came in and that is just when the girl next door called her and she went to see what she wanted; but all the time she really wanted to let her know that some thing was about to happen and she need help. So she went back in and begins to talk to Larry and begin to say things about her and her ex-husband being back together and other things. He told her that he had seen her and him having sex. Then he begin to tell her all he wanted was to have sex with her one last time; little did angel know that this would turn out to be one of his famous lines every time she put him out; or when she did not want to have sex with him this is what he would use or he would tell her that she did not want to have sex with him because she was having it with some one else.

This was the kind of manipulating thing he would do to her in order to get his way. And like a dummy she would go along with it out of fear of what he would do if she did not go along with it.

Angel thought she had a little more carriage because she know what he was suppose to do the first time; so she thought she would give it a try; after all if her son could stand up for her why could she not stand up for her self. So she told him she had to got next door for some thing; so when she went to go out the door and try to escape he grabbed her and pick her up and closed the door and started beating her in the face and all she could do was call on the name of Jesus ever time he hit her. And all the girl next door could do was stand on the other side of the door and listen to the licks he was passing. After he got through hitting her he got his paper off the floor and ran out the back door. Well she got up and brushed her self off and went next door. By this time they had called the police but angel did not press charge because she know what she was dealing with was not a normal human being but a spirit demon also.

He even had the nerve to come back after the police left talking about he wanted his stuff animals. So she gave them to him. She knows that this would not be the end of this. Her twin brother was now hanging around because her ex-husband and him got high together; but they where not there when it happen. They where out some where getting high because Odie had come into some money from when he got his finger shot off. So that night when they did come in and saw what had happen to angel it was on. They went looking for him that night I don't know if they caught him but the next day angel and her brother went down to 13th and Michigan to press charges against him. It would be here that angel would take a picture of her first and last black eye. And they did issues a warrant against him and she had and orders of protection.

Some how the minute she got home he was around the building and when she stop the police and showed them her papers they had a few words with him and that was it. Angel family did go looking for him and then Larry called the police on her family; because he came driving up in the car and one of her nephew came out the house with a bat and started busing out his car windows and angel will never for get the look on his face of fear that he had once given her. Then he turned around and bust out the house windows with a brick. But when it was time to go to court because he had pressed charges against her brother and ex-husband; so when they got to court he got in front of the judge and lied on her husband to try and have him locked up and it would almost work, because he had just got out of jail. After this angel stayed away for Larry until she discovered that he was stalking her still. Angel was going to school she was attending Olive-Harvey College so she could obtain a degree in criminal justice now was the time for it. She still found her self back with Larry was not love she know she did not what it was. He seen to come around when some thing was wrong in her life and some how he would be there. Even though she broke up with him she felt they could some how be friends but it would take her ten years to find out that this was another one of his skims to get back with her; or in her house every time he was put out and it worked for ten years.

She could still remember the time when Larry would stalk her at the church. So she went to the pastor during the service to get help because he had come to the church to see her. And upon telling the pastor, even with the black eye he had given her for every one to see, all the pastor could tell her at the end of the service was that he had made Larry a promise that she would call him. Angel could not believe what she was hearing from this pastor. It would not belong when God would tell her to live this church and go to another one.

Not based on the fact that he was not at hearing to her situation but because it was time for her to leave. God was taking her to a new level.

With in these two year angel would go through and learn a lot of things about life and men and what God meant when he said take up your cross and follow me; and when he said that the road would not be easy; but I would not put more on you than you can bare. Angel kindness was being taking for a weakness and the enemy would try to use this for the next ten years to bring angel down.

But as a Christian angel would have to endure the heart ship of a good soldier and it would not be easy. She would be lied on, cheated on, beat on, push around and almost killed. But as she had learned faith is the substance of thing hope for the evidence of things not seen. All she has was in the word of God.

Angel experience for the next ten years would be like a baby trying to learn how to walk. It would take time to come out of these things she had got her self into; but every time she would look for what it was the God had for her to learn. She was determined to triumph over the enemy. Whether it was how people work, or how the enemy works, even when it came to learning the mistakes she was constantly making. She would also learn what gifts God had given her and would learn the difference between the work of the enemy and the work of God. In do time angel would learn that the enemy will even try to falsify him self as an angel of light. Some thing angel had never thought to look for before. She would have to learn all the tricks of the enemy and how they worked and when he would use them against her.

God had given angel a gift to see thing before they happen and some of the things that took place she know would happen and because she did not really understand what was happening. Then even if she did; could she prevent what was happen to her; when she saw these things coming? She could even tell Larry what he was going to say; if for her use and when it would come to pass she would now have a better understanding of what God was trying to show her. God would give her insight into the spirit realm. The bible sat tries the spirit by the spirit but with him that was to do. Because he had a lying spirit. There were some things angel did not understand at this time and one of them was what she keep returning to the same state. This is what she was trying to find out; and discover was that yes God wanted her to get along with her enemies and even learn to love them. But the bible also says that God would not have us ignored of the enemy devices. She was still learning about God the father and his son and his word there was still some things she needed to know. So she dedicated most of her time to learning to word and reading the word some more. Because even though you know some of the word God can give you a different revelation ever time. She was up against something that she needed to know about that she was not in the flesh. Angel felt at time God really has some special he wanted her to do because of the turmoil she was going through not that she wasn't adding to it. It was as if she had known control when it came to not letting him back in. Once he was back in her house it was like an alarm won't off and she would woke-up; but it would be to late then or she would say things she meant but did not mean. A double-minded man is unstable in all his ways. And at this time this is how she felt.

Angel remembers the time when Larry had put some eye drops in her drink to put her to sleep. Angel did not sit to well with it because when she found out about it. For once she was going to do to him what he had done to her. She went and borrowed some eye drops and now she would find out if it really work; and she did and it does work because that night Larry set in the car and went to sleep with the windows up in it and angel set there and watched him go to sleep. It was in the summer time so before he got fully asleep angel woke him up so that he would know that she was not the one. But he never said any thing about it but she know that he knew what had happen; what he did done to her had been done to him; so he came in the house and poured out his drink he had in the refrigerator.

This gave him some thing to think about but it did not stop him from trying to control her. He knows that ever round angel was getting stronger because she would do some thing that would show him she was. Angel was paying all the bills and buying all the food in her house. Except when he knows she could not afford to then he would. All Larry did was ate, sleep and ran the streets. But there would come a time when she would tell him that if he wanted to continue to live in her house he would have to pay some rent.

She was not longer going to pay for him to lie up in her house. Well Larry did start paying a little rent, but did not last long and angel still found her self back where she started paying bills and buying food. Any thing Larry gave her he made sure he got that back and some. The bad part about this was that angel know al these things but yet did nothing about what she know was happen; she just let Larry think that he was getting over on her. But then to she know that vengeance belong to God and even thing he took form her god would give it back and more.

After about two years of living on seventy second street angel went thorough many other things that would make her strong. Some time she often wonder about that because she kept finding her self-back in the same old place. Places God had just go her out of; why was she doing things she really did not want to do when it came to Larry. Angel remember the time when she asked Larry to leave again and he told her that he wasn't going no where and if he could not leave there neither was she. So again she went and told her nephew and what he had said and what did she do that for because she know her nephews would be glade to get him something they had been waiting for, and that is just what happen. When her nephew say him drive up he came out the house with a bat and before he could even get out of the car he took the bat and bust the car window and told him to get out the car. Larry was afraid at this time and would not get out the car. So what he did was go to the other side of the car and got out and ran down the streets to flag the police down. And because he did not see one at that time he came back and it would be at this time her son would come out the house with a gun and put it to Larry face and tell him he should kill him, not knowing that the gun had know bullets in it because one of her other nephews had taking the bullets out of it the day before because he had given the gun to Angel to protect her self with knowing that she would really use it because she was not that kind of person and she did not have the nerve to.

So Angel ran out the house to stop her son and Larry would not stop there; he went and got some of his family members so that he could get some of his things. Well Angel thank God that know one got hurt. So things die down and Larry stayed away for a while. But other things where happen in Angel life with her oldest son. By this time Eric Jr. had gotten him self on drugs and was staying trouble. One of her other brothers would come and stay with her because he needed a place to stay because things where not going so well with him and the relationship he was in. Angel apartment was the one place her brothers and nephews know they could come and stay it; and most of the time that is what they did. When they needed a baby sitter they would bring the kids to Angel. Angel did not have a problem with this because she loved taking care of children. Considering what her childhood was like so it was her heart to take care of her nieces because most of them at this time was girls.

Well some more time would pass and odie would try to make his way back but Angel know that this would not work because nothing had change. How she would know this was one night when they where at her sister house and some how that bible came into a conversation they had; had and he was drunk and talking crazy. And he got angry and upset with Angel and it was from this point that Angel know that she was not going to get back with him know matter what happen. But she also know that she did not want Larry back; but her action did not match her words.

Because there had come a time when Angel oldest son had gotten him self into some trouble and because Larry know the guys he was able to stop them form killing him like they had intended to. So this would cause Angel to have compassion on him and let him back into her house once again. No the smart thing to but she did.

Not only that because she was paying rent to a landlord in cash and he was know turning the money in she would soon have to go court to be evicted. She did not know what Larry was going to do but she would have to got back to her mother house. But a little before that her sister would have to move also for what ever reason she did not know.

So in the mean time Angel would move back to her mother house and Larry would find him some where to stay.

So Angel would go to her sister house after she found her some where to stay in the mist of going over there she would met a young man in store down the street. Not that she was really interested in him but her sister know him and she would talk to him from time to time.

Well after a while of going over there she would give the guy her phone number and they would talk from time to time and then she would manage to go on a day with him hoping the Larry would not find out but there was very little he did not know how he was knowing she would never know. But they went to the museum one day and they had a nice time with her youngest son Odie Jr. some how the word got back to Larry. And he would bring it to her attention that he know. But she would only deny it.

About six months of living in her mother house and looking for a apartment Angel brother Willie would some how manage to get the apartment up stairs from her sister. But it was only suppose to be her and him. Angel brother had told her that if she moved Larry in that he would not stay in the apartment. But things would not turn out like that Larry would be moving in and within four months Angel brother would move out and leave her in the apartment with Larry. Then it would be Larry that would cause Angel to have to move out even though; when she looked at the situation he was right to get on the landlord for not fixing up the apartment and it rained in the front room from the ceiling. So because they did not want to fix Angel would have to move. But before this had happen Angel had put a plan be in place in cause this should happen. Because Section 8, had given angel an apartment in the projects with rent that was less than one hundred. so she had tried to get Larry to go and move in the apartment so he could have some where to stay instead of living there but he was not going for it want she what she was doing.

So often Larry had made trouble for angel in this apartment she just went on and told the landlord that she was going to move. And she did; she would now move in the projects in the place she had tried to get Larry to move in. it was now 1995, and angel was in school still she had not given up on her dreams and she was going for her degree, this would take some of the stress off her mind of what she was going there. Even she did not know how she was doing it; it could have been nobody but God keeping her that she was not confused about. But she wold go on to graduate and get her degree. While going to school she would also get a part-time job in the school and this would help do a little more for the kids and the house. But many other things would happen while living in this apartment. Angel felt that she was getting a little stronger about the situations that was going on in her life. In the mist of going to school she would met a man that worked in the school and it happen when she would go and get things Xeroxed and he would appeared to be a nice man. So he would grow on Angel and again she would seize the opportunity to get to know him. Not realizing that you can not really get to know some one that you haven" really spent know time with. so she would fabricate the truth a little bit to tell this man that she was not in a real relationship. So this man would bring her home one time and one night unexpected this man showed up at her house unannounced and Larry would open the door and tell her that some one was at the door for her. what to her surprise it was him; he had taking it upon him self to come to her house only to have to leave after being invited in for a minute. What was he thinking to come to her house. what would Larry do to her after he had left. Even thought he was doing things him self. So after these man left Larry went into his question mode of who was that and what was he doing coming to the house. Angel manage to tell some story and Larry would some what believe but not believe it because he know better. After all he was a expert on lying and he know a lie for the truth. How was she going to face this man again; what would she tell him. after all he was in the wrong he had know business coming to her house unannounced. But some how things would pass over and she would keep on seeing him but not at he house. there would be times when she would go to his house. She never saw him unless it was at work and they would go to his house for lunch and that would be it. with the exception she went to his house one time he had invited her to met his sister and they set and talked for a little while than Angel would leave.

It would be in this apartment that things would be a little better but not much.

Angel would find her self confused at time with Larry because he wanted a child not that she know he had kids already other then the ones she know about. But she would have to take care of any of them in this apartment.

The argue to get out was becoming stronger and stronger and now was the time to be thinking about how God would get her out. Was it time. Angel could remember one time when she left her apartment and went to live with her mother after Larry begin to go with the girl next door right in front of her face. And there was another time when he said that he was going to pay cards at one of he girlfriends house as usual and this time angel would go looking for him to see if he was doing what he said. And when she arrived at the place where he was suppose to be she found him at the table talking to one of the girl about having sex with her after she got drunk. He did not know angel was standing at the door. So she let him know that she heard what he had said and then she left and when home. It would be at this time that she would tell him that she was going to her mother house to stay; and that he could stay in the apartment. Not only for this reason but because some one had shot in the window when they where not at home. And she did not know if it was gang related or something meant for Larry. But she was not going to stay to find out. So she did what she usually do and that was to take off. But this time now her son was getting him self deeper and deeper in trouble with gang and drugs.

In June of 1995, Angel would receive her degree in Criminal Justice but she would not stop there. Neither would she give up on God she would more involved in the church learning all that she could. Even if she had to get on the bus and go her desire to seek God had grown strong because she know that she would need all that God had for her and some. Angel was learning how to believe in God, trust him, pray to him, worship him, and how the enemy worked. She could truly say that this place God had sent her to she was learning a lot. Even though there where some things that trouble her she could not let that get her off focus. She had to keep her focus on God.

The abuse was easing up for Angel but the mental abuse was still in the air. There would be time when she would wonder if the things that Larry was saying was true. But then she to keep in mind that Larry was a compulsive liar, and he had a way of making a lie look like the true even though she must admit some times he was right, but majority of the he was wrong. When she wasn't doing any thing he would say she was and when she wasn't he would say she was so either way it went he had to be right at all time. He was doing so much until he would take what he was doing and making look like some one else was doing it. and he did not have a problem telling what he was doing but it was how he told what he was doing and he change what the person was to him that he was doing it with. Well after about a year or so in this place Angel would soon be moving because they where getting ride of the projects and Angel would have to move. So she went looking for another apartment.

She know that she did not want Larry to move with her but the chance of that where second to none. But she would give it a try.

Time was passing and Angel was not getting ready to move; she will never forget that day in turmoil as what she should do with Larry things. Because he had went to work that morning yes work! he had a little job working in a clothing store with his one of his friends that he know. And on this morning while he went to work Angel would be trying to figure out what was she going to do with his things. God send me a sign she keep telling herself that morning. She would even seek a sign for the movers that had came to move her things. So I leave his thing or take them with me she asked the movers. Well they where know real help; so she would have to make a decision on her own one the could cost her but that is a chance she would be willing to take. So she did; she left Larry things in the apartment in hopes that know one would go in and take any thing. Because it could mean trouble for her.

So she move but there was know peace she just know that he would find her. so way some how he would. And he did when the women from had to come inspect the place had knock on the door not knowing that Larry was with her. when angel open the door she would the shock of her life. What she had been wonding all day had now come to pass.

Larry walked in with this stupid look on his face and Angel asking him what are you doing here. Telling him; he needed to go to the old place and get his things out of there. Knowing he had know help and again manipulating her. I need you take me get my things and where am I going to take them, I don't have know place to go he tells Angel.

The same things she had left she now had to go back and help him get. Not all that he had would come to Angel house but some things was to much. Again he was in but even he would see that she was getting stronger in her decision making. It some courage to leave his things in the apartment; knowing the type of person he was.

It would be at this time that Angel would begin to express her feeling she could know longer hold in.

So things would go good for a minute then they would go back to the same things of his accusing her. But God was giving her some insight to Larry and his tacket, plots, and plans. So he really could not get to her like he use to. But this did not stop him from doing what he do best and that was go out and find young girls half his age with disables and use them for what he wanted to make him self look good. And he even got in good with the people up stairs.

At this time Angel would buy her a piece of car to get around in and she would continue her education. So it would be at this time that she would go back to college and get another degree. Chicago State University. Yet in still her oldest son was still set in his ways and doing the same things but only getting worse. Angel tried to get him to give his life to God, she even got him to go to church a couple of times but that did not help him. at this time he had a girlfriend and they where getting along as long as he was not getting into trouble or in jail. But this would soon die out. Angel even brought him a car but that did not last long because a month after he got the car he tour it up, how is another story that only he can tell. But she had to be able to say that she tried to do something right. Angel know her children were not happy with the relationship she was in but what could they do it was between Angel and God now.

It would be at this time that after a few encounters with Larry that she would soon turn it over to God and let him work it out. She would just tried to keep a peace of mind know matter what happen.

Besides her children needed her more then what she was going through. Her youngest son was growing older now and he was begin to do things for him self, he even went out and got him self a job. Some thing his older brother had not done yet. Odie Jr. was now becoming a man. Even though his hobbies where strange to Angel. As she set in this smoked filled room she tried to remember when did he want to become a dancer. So had been so caught up in what was going on with her that she could not even remember when or how. But she was glade to see that the things that she was going through had know killed his dreams and goals. He would even go on to finish high school and graduate. And his mother would be there for him.

Shortly after that Angel would go on to graduate for the Chicago State her self. But in between time some other things would happen. See Larry never stop doing what he was doing and there would be time when Angel would think to her self that may be this was the person for her because she could not get rid of him. But he would manage to kill that thought every time.

One winter day Angel had given Larry her car to use to go out and do what ever it was he do. So when she went to her car after words what would she find near her car. A condom and she know that her son did not do it; it had to be him. then there would be other things that would show up.

He would now got to the ex-stream of talking about her to the people up stairs and Angel know that they where having a field day with him and what he was saying about her.

But she could not let that get the best of her; it was his insecurity getting the best of him. even the he would obtain a job for a couple of months.

Angel could remember the time when he would go with her step-sister and one of her cousin and it would come out. It was in the winter time when she found out; so she got her nephew to come and change the locks on the door and pack his things so when he came from off the rid he took with her cousin he would be leaving she did not car if it was winter he had to go know question asked. Well angel waited for him to show up and he did only to find out that it was time for him to go. So again she would have to help him take his things over to his mother house and leave. This would last for a while and Angel would obtain a job at UPS. In 1999, and she would have some day that she did not care to remember. Because Larry would revert back to some of his old ways. She could remember the time when he would stalk her at work and one night he even embarrassed her as she was on her way into work. he met her at the car and told her what he was going to do to her. so not knowing what to do she follow her wrong mind and decided to go to the gas station trying to play it off. And once they got to the gas station he put a knife to her neck and told her that he should kill her and leave her right there.

There was nothing she could say or do but tell him do go head and do what he was going to do. Because she was not going to keep on being afraid of him. But once again God stop the death Angel and she went to work not that he was not there when she got off. Because he had gotten him a piece of car so he could get around to stalk her ever move.

But Angel had to go on in the name of Jesus; through fear and trembling. So soon Larry would get his own apartment with the help of Angel. In hope that he would now leave her alone.

But you know how that work he wanted to have his cake and eat it to. Even though there would be times when Angel found her self calling him on her way home. She it was because she had been accused and stalked so long until it had become apart of her to let him know what she was doing.

The job she had did not pay much but it was something because she needed all she could to pay the bills and buy food for house. She was still trying to make ends met. But she was making the best of it. During this time

Angel would met some one else while going to school and he would be a police officer and Angel would go to his house from time to time he even told Angel that she could move in if she wanted to. At this time he was living alone and really had know on special. Angel never seize the opportunity to do, but she would wish that she would have.

This friendship would be off and on because of Angel insecurities and of his not really wanting to give up his pass with women. So they would just see each other from time to time. Even though there was some things Angel did and did not like about him.

She would remember the time when Angel would call him and tell him that what they where doing would have to stop. Because of what she was going through with Larry and it would be at this time that she would discover that he had some type of feelings for her because he asked her to come over and talk to him before she made any decision.